Eating Is Sacred

Eating Is Sacred

Yayasan Misi Belas Kasihan

TA MARIANTHONY

Mercy Mission Foundation

DATUK ANN MARIANTHONY

PARTRIDGE

A Penguin Random House Company

To order additional copies of this book, contact
Toll Free 800 101 2657 (Singapore)
Toll Free 1 800 81 7340 (Malaysia)
orders.singapore@partridgepublishing.com

www.partridgepublishing.com/singapore

Contents

"People are fed by the Food Industry, Which pays no attention to HEALTH"

and are treated by the health industry, which pays no attention to FOOD." – Wendell Berry

Dear Owner of SACRED EATING,

Congratulations on taking the first step to peak performance of mind, body and soul. We are so pleased that you have decided to take control of your health and purchased this book.

We're confident you will find this unique book and the simple yet powerful health information you are to gain will benefit you and your loved ones. This book contains the simplest beneficial component for your overall health and wellness endeavors.

Unlike other books out there today, we intend to give we a range of perfect health solutions that cuts to the chase – separating fact from fiction – and provide us with unbiased information on critical men's and women's healthy eating issues… the latest breakthroughs in Naturopathy diet, fitness, and nutrition… as well as simple guidance to help us achieve our health goals whatever that may be.

We aim to bust popular myths and provide you with a discreet guide for becoming stronger, healthier, sharper, leaner, more energetic and feeling years younger in mind, body and spirit.

Our diverse team at **TA MARIANTHONY MERCY MISSION FOUNDATION** is committed to a "no holds-barred" approach of reporting our unique health viewpoints – and sometimes controversial philosophies. Each and every book hereafter, gives us something actionable to keep for good or give away to our loved ones. You'll get authorized valuable insights from our team who are continually breaking new ground with our own research in Naturopathy health training, supplements and nutrition… our dedicated research team with approaches that has been tested on ourselves…. And who have taken the spiritual path to reach weight loss goals and regain a healthy lifestyle…….

Our philosophy is, "we only live once so make sure we live life to its fullest…"

We believe that living a healthy, enriched life goes hand-in-hand with food from nature's pharmacy and getting peak performance for our mind, body and soul – and the fact that we can truly change all that we do, and all that we are.

Our goal is to give you the best health information available, to help you live life to its fullest potential.

Our ultimate goal eventually is for you to attain optimal state of health just by eating right.

Spread the good news about good health! Tell a friend about this book by **TA MARIANTHONY MERCY MISSION FOUNDATION.**

Yours for health, success and happiness!

COACH PRAKASH CHRISTIANSEN – prakash.christiansen@gmail.com
DATUK RADHA RAVI – kingpin1953@gmail.com
CELINE GAYATHREE GIVANATHAN – gaya3_1485@yahoo.com
DATUK ANN MARIANTHONY – tresa18@gmail.com

Acknowledgement

COACH PRAKASH CHRISTIANSEN, without him this book would have never made it to your hands. Writing a book was the last thing on my mind, till I met him. He subtly persuaded me to put this book together. He constantly monitored my progress, periodically followed up, checked my work and gently reminded me of datelines. I thank him for his encouragement at every stage of this book and the faith he had in me. I am obligated to him for life.

MARY ANTHONY, my mother from whom I inherited the gift of giving. I am extremely grateful to her for being able to give with love and without expectation.

DATUK SUBRAYAN SELLAPPAN, who believed in me and supported in the formation of TAMMMF. I am indebted to him in many ways.

DATUK RADHA RAVI, I had used him as collateral on many occasions. Many a times, his face value mattered and he had willingly obliged. I thank him for being there.

MY MASTER DHYAN VIMAL, who dissected and showed me to me. He embedded this bible verse into the depth of me, *"Honor all people, Love the brotherhood, Fear God, Honor the King, Servants and be submissive to your Masters with all fear, not only to the good and gentle, but also to the harsh" (Peter: 2:17-18). Master,* I bow to you, thank you and love you more and forever.

VELLARSAMY VEMAN, my friend who selflessly shared so much of health information with me. I am extremely grateful and obligated to him for providing me with lots of useful information.

V.KUNDASAMY, Words are just not enough to express my sincere gratitude for all his kindness, support and assistance during the initial stages of TAMMMF.

CELINE GAYATHREE, I thank my daughter for all her constructively critical suggestions and corrections of my work. She waited up with me every night. We constantly debated on certain topics till we decided on the most appropriate answer. I must thank her for the many cups of coffee that she made me throughout the completion of this book.

MASTER VENUGOPAL – My dearest of dear friends. Our friendship had survived all kinds of adversities. With you Master, friendship does not have the same and ordinary meaning anymore. I thank you for being there.

REKO RAJU – K-Link Crown Ambassador, I thank him for all his support during my peak times as a Health Advisor. You are my inspiration and I am indebted to you in many ways. Thank you.

VASANTHI NAIDU – President of The Shelter Home for Abused Women and Children, Seremban. She is a multi talented divine individual who inspired me in many different ways. She is one great friend at this very moment. Thank you.

My sincere gratitude to these special people who chose to stand by me and encouraged me directly or indirectly namely, **STEPHEN MATTHEWS, THIRUNIKANTHAN, SURESH PALANIAPPAN, RACHEL GOMEZ, ASHA RAVINDRAN, PREMA SUBRAMANIAM** (DECEASED), **DANIEL SATHESKUMARAN, YB RAVI MUNUSAMY, DATUK PADUKA HABIBAH, DR AZAHAR, JULIANA SHARINA JAYABALAN** and the real-life Angel of my life **S KAVERY RAVEE** and her charming husband **ACR MAJOR DR RAVEE.**

I pay homage to my late brother **CAPTAIN EDWARD FRANCIS MARIANTHONY** who inspired me to take up Naturopathy as my profession.

I pay my respect to my late maternal uncle **P.ANTHONYSAMY** who thought me that self respect, honor and dignity are not to be compromised.

Finally I dedicate this work to my Father, **D. MARIANTHONY** who is the prime reason for all my success.

Datuk Ann Marianthony

Naturopathy Eating Habits

Definition by way of eating habits

	Activities According to Guna-s	TAMASIC Harm Based (WEAK)	RAJASIC Self Based (COWARD)	SATTVIC Love Based (WINNER)
1	Long term Goals:	Are to sleep, eat & destroy others	Are for personal pleasure, prestige, power & wealth	Are for unity, love & welfare of all
2.	Attachments to:	Has false beliefs and delusion	Is attached to action and desire to acquire worldly objects and recognition.	Would like happiness & "True" knowledge for all
3.	Actions:	Acts without due thought about the results, or how his actions are carried out. Denies all responsibility and may indulge in criminal or violent activities to harm others or himself. Has no humility and often procrastinates	Every activity is performed with arrogance, pomp & big show; often for selfish reasons to gain personal possessions, prestige, power and wealth. These activities create anxieties, agitation, bitterness, conflict & anger which may lead to sorrow & depression.	Unbiased and actions are without likes & dislikes for the action or the people involved and there is no insistence on a particular result. Activities are carried out according to Dharma, peace and welfare of all. *Sattvic* person remains calm and composed in success or failure.

4.	Type of food:	Eats tasteless, stale, preserved, decomposed or polluted food.	Prefers spicy, bitter, sour, salty or very hot food	Eats nutritious food that increases life and strength and promotes purity of thoughts,
5.	Feelings of cook:	Cook has negative feelings of anger, hate, loathe, detest, etc	Thinks about "what will I get out of this activity?	Cook has love in her heart and wants to share the food with all.
6.	Place of Dining:	Eats in bar filled with smoke	Likes fancy restaurants	Person prefers to eat at home or in temple.
7.	Quantity of food consumed:	Consumes a lot of food	Eats a lot only if he likes the food	Will eat just enough to maintain healthy body.
8.	Time for food:	Eats at irregular hours or eats lying down	Eats while, talking, working, walking or watching TV	Eats quietly, slowly, regularly
9.	Drink:	Takes recreational drugs and drinks alcoholic beverages	Drinks excitable caffeinated beverages	Prefers water, fruit juice etc.
10.	Sleep:	Sleeps during the day or while at work.	Has difficulty sleeping and has excitable dreams.	Enjoys restful, sound sleep.
11.	Speech:	Talks without thinking, tells lies, complains about everything, criticizes, uses obscene language. Disrespectful to older persons	Talks about "I, me &, mine" all the time.	Thinks & tells the truth (*satyam*) in pleasant words (*priyam*) and what is beneficial to all (*hitam*). Speech is encouraging and uplifting.

12.	Buddhi (Intellect):	Thinks that which is morally and ethically "right" is "wrong" & what is "wrong" is "right".	Is confused about what is "right" and what is "wrong". He cannot decide what to do when there is a moral dilemma.	Knows "right" from "wrong", what is according to dharma, and what is good for all and brings long-term security.
13.	Pleasure is derived from:	Person feels happy after getting up late in the morning, after getting intoxicating drinks, doing harm to others, and destruction of property.	Feels happy during activities that give pleasure derived from sense gratification. Activity feels like fun in the beginning but ends in grief later (*preyas*).	Involves in activities that are good for all. This may be difficult in the beginning but brings long lasting pleasure & peace to all (*shreyas*).
14.	Keeps Company of:	Prefers the company of criminals	Keeps company of people who will help him achieve his selfish goals to become rich and famous.	Keeps company of good people (*satsang*) who live according to *Dharma*.
15.	Reading, Listening to Music and Watching Movies:	Likes trashy, vulgar & violent entertainment.	Prefers exciting literature and movies.	Reads, listens and watches value based entertainment.

16.	Rituals:	Performs religious ceremony without faith & knowledge about meaning of mantras or rituals, to gain power over others, harm others, get strength or wealth to destroy others, to torture their own body and without giving *dakshina* (gift to God)	Performs rituals to gain personal prestige, profit or power. *Dakshina* is given to *God* to show off wealth and self satisfaction.	Performs obligatory rituals with proper understanding of the meaning of mantras, without expecting any personal gain, and resolve to put them in practice. Generous *dakshina* is given with love and respect.
17.	Charity (Dana):	Does not believe in giving any charity or it is given to unworthy cause or without love and respect.	Has a condition when giving. Regrets when he has to give *Dana* or gives to gain something in return.	Gives willingly with faith, to the right cause, as a sense of duty and without expectation of getting anything in return.
18.	Knowledge:	Does not have any understanding of the "Truth" (God).	Cannot discriminate "right" from "wrong". He thinks of all life forms as separate from each other and different from himself. Other peoples believe are discriminated and disrespected.	Feels that the same "God", *"Paramatma"* (life force) lives in the whole universe.

19.	Three Characters (brothers) from Ramayana:	Character of *Kumbhakarna* who slept for six months, ate for six months and fought against *Rama.*	Brother of *Ravana.* He was very intelligent, knowledgeable, strong and brave but had weakness for *Sita* who was married to *Rama.*	Brother of *Vibhishana.* He left *Ravana* and joined forces with *Rama* to fight with his brother *Ravana* who abducted *Sita.*
20.	*Tava* (Disciplined Effort):	Performs *Tava* with the goal of doing harm to others or for torturing himself.	Performs *Tava* for gaining respect, power or wealth.	Performs *Tava* to worship *devas* with faith and unselfish motive.
21.	Temperament:	Is lethargic and vengeful	Is restless and ambitious	Is calm and focused
22.	Tyaga (renunciation of fruits of action:	Does not carry out his duties because of ignorance or laziness.	Does not perform his duties because of fear of outcome of the action or if the task is unpleasant or difficult.	Performs duties without expecting anything in return.
23.	Worship:	Worships ghosts.	Worships *Yaksha-s* & *Rakshaksa-s*	Worships God.

Naturopathy way of Eating is Spiritual

Eating is a sacred act because food gives life. Food is entirely a gift to self. Eating is the one activity that brings every being on the planet in touch with their health and desires every day. Plants get their food directly from the sun, but humans must eat other living things to survive. We should remember that every time we eat, a plant or animal sacrifices its life. This is why many of us practice thanksgiving before eating; we thank the Creator for the abundance and the life of the food.

We have been taught that, "We are what we eat". We have heard this over and over again but do we really understand its actual meaning? When making food choices, we need to select foods that will help us evolve into a higher state of consciousness. We need to understand and be sure the energy from the food we eat is used for the greater goodness that is meant. Red meat such as beef and pork encourage egotistical behavior and domination. According to Naturopathy, pure nutritious foods like fish, grains, raw fruits and vegetables help us let go and surrender to an energy level of a higher power.

We MUST Feel the After-Meals Joy

Digestion and Blood Flow are partners in Good Health.

On an average, digestion takes up to 60% of our daily metabolism. The fluids used in digestion, together with the energy for digestion is provided by our blood. Therefore, digestion depends strongly on the blood and its circulation to the digestive organs. For this reason, even minor tasks, sullen state of mind, anger, bad mood, depression, stress, anxiety and even conversations while eating pulls blood away from digestion. Hence digestion becomes sluggish. That's why it is very important that we be in a calm and relaxed state when we eat. Some foods, like very cold drinks and ice creams, causes restricted blood flow to the stomach. We must avoid all foods and activities that will divert blood from the digestive tract while eating and during assimilation.

The first fifteen minutes after eating are very crucial. Rest is recommended. The substantial increase in blood flow to the digestive tract brings about fluid to acid-producing glands that lines the stomach. This is when the corresponding lack of blood in the brain makes us feel sleepy. It's important to relax during this time of sleepiness, even to the point of reclining on the left side. Humans should surrender to digestion, giving the digestive system and the body the time, space and blood it needs to correctly and completely digest food. After the stomach fills with fluids, blood will be released for other activities in our body. Energy and alertness will return to the mind. Then only, the afternoon siesta ends and we are ready to reclaim the day. This is why we must never overeat. Overeating causes the digestive energy to focus too long in our stomach causing much discomfort.

Habits that needs to be cultivated to improve blood flow and digestion:

- Wait for the signs of true hunger
- Eat the same time every day. Our stomach loves to be on schedule.
- A simple glass of room temperature water twenty minutes before a meal can improve digestive functions by as much as 30%.
- Be in a relaxed state while eating and for fifteen minutes afterwards.
- Eat simple food combinations
- Avoid ice cold drinks or ice cold food.
- Pamper the digestion after a tough day with tested nourishing soups
- Completely chew and mix food with saliva before swallowing.
- Always fill stomach 1/3 full with food, 1/3 with water, and leave 1/3 empty
- Eat a simple "1st meal", a light "2nd meal", and a gentle "3rd meal".

Really warm (nearly hot) soups prevent Dry Stomach Syndrome. Our stomach likes green tea, roobois tea, steamed veggies and soups. Our stomach struggles with raw food, very cold food, tough food, preserved food and excessively irritating foods like too much chilies. Our stomachs struggle even more with overeating and too many varieties of food that is haphazardly prepared in the name of love.

Improper Eating Habits

Over eating, irregular and improper eating habits lead to poor digestion, assimilation and absorption of food. Our average core body temperature must be 37°C for optimum digestive functions. The body temperature plays a vital role in digestion. It is important to understand, protect and maintain our body temperature at all times as the right body temperature fuels and nourishes the blood and all other metabolic activity. Poor digestion leads to formation of altered blood chemistry. In addition to administering the principles above, here are some more habits to avoid:

- Snacking between meals
- Eating excess fats, proteins, sweets, sour, and salty foods
- Eating heavy food late at night / sleeping immediately after eating (at least 2 hours between a meal and sleep).
- Eating too much or too soon after a meal. At least 4 hours between meals is recommended (best to wait till hungry).
- Eating while being constipated, suffering gassy stomach, frequent burping, or eating during any other digestive distress.

We tend to struggle when it comes to Good eating Habits

A poor diet is one that's nutritionally deficient. Most of us might not be aware that we practice bad diet habits every day, regardless of the variety and amount of food we eat. A good diet focuses more on quality than quantity. The causes of a bad diet are common yet overlooked, as many of us think we are eating a healthy, nutritious diet when we in fact do otherwise. The reasons mainly being;

Commercialism

These days almost all food is readily available for immediate consumption and is prepackaged for our convenience. Most of these foods have no nutritional value whatsoever. Food that's marketed as "a healthy snack" or a "perfect meal all on its own" very rarely has anything else other than sugar and chemical flavors, with very little of the vitamins and nutrients that it markets. In addition, many of us include fast food in our diet, and that's full of low-density lipoproteins, trans-fats and cholesterol, three components that are bad for anyone's health. Many of us eat "commercialized" food every day. This clearly contributes to a bad diet and unhealthy eating.

Poor Eating Habits

We tend to live on quick grabs like "roti canai", "Chapattis" and expensive wonder foods that are hyped up by some money motivated industry. We tend to hold on to Stone Age belief that breakfast lunch and dinner is a must whether or not we are hungry. There are other times that we have two meals at once simply because we had missed the earlier meal. The number of meals we have a day truly depends on how active we are physically. There is no such thing as the most important meal of the day. Any meal when we are hungry is an important meal. Some people say that they skip meals in order to lose weight while some overeat to gain weight. Again, it needs to be stressed that no one can actually skip a meal and really suffer hunger pangs. When hunger strikes, each cell in our body is given a "danger" signal for preparation to switch to survival mode. We become dysfunctional until we eat something. It is a meaningless understatement to say that one can skip meals and go on with doing other things. In some instances, it is meant that the normal conventional meal is replaced with chapatti, noodles, soups, whole meal bread etc. because it is believed that oily food is unhealthy.

For decades now, saturated fats have been unfairly vilified in the media. While we have, as a nation, reduced our fat consumption steadily for the past few decades, obesity, diabetes, and heart diseases have still skyrocketed. Medical centers are a rapidly growing market. How do we explain this? These dieters pay no attention to the food's nutritional value and long-term adverse effects. Poor eating habits have a great impact on our health and can be the major cause of a bad diet and illnesses that follows.

A healthy diet consists of a complete meal with the daily nutritional requirement, full of fiber, vitamins and minerals that maintain the human body inside and out. The key point to be remembered all the time is that we must have a balanced meal. Typical, simple example of a complete meal no matter who we are is:

1 part carbohydrate i.e. rice, bread, toast etc
(2 tbsp rice)
1 part protein i.e. meat or fish or egg
(the size of our fist / 3 eggs or 6 egg whites)
3 parts vegetable
(3 cups vegetable)
1 part fruit
(1 whole apple or any fruit the size of an apple)

Note: For optimum digestion, eat the fruit first, wait for an hour, then eat the vegetable and after 2 hours, follow on with the protein and lastly the carbohydrate.

Poor Health Education

The lack of knowledge on what a good diet is, leads people into following a diet that doesn't meet the recommended daily requirement of vitamins, minerals and nutrients that our body needs. Many people are sickly and malnourished without even knowing it because of our lack of education as to what a good diet really is.

Lifestyle

Everyone's perception of healthy lifestyle differs. Even people who typically follow a healthy, well balanced diet may fall into a bad diet category due to change of environment, stress and physical changes. For instance, women should adjust their diet during menstruation since they have an increased need for iron and calcium. Normally healthy people who follow a good diet are also prone to a bad diet when they're under heavy pressure, stress or when they undergo a drastic change in their work place or at home, such as excessive work load, moving places of employment or residence or loss of a loved one.

The Fact about Oil in Food

As a matter of fact, saturated fat plays a number of critical roles in the body. The membrane of every cell in our body is made of fat – more than 10,000,000,000 of them. These membranes are at least 50% saturated fat. Our body needs membranes that are strong and supple to keep toxins out of cells, to facilitate nutrients moving in and circulating and to keep the internal cellular signaling working optimally. Our brain is also made mostly of fat too. Saturated fat protects our liver from alcohol and other toxins we all allow to dwell within our modern lifestyles. And our lungs and kidneys cannot function without fat. Saturated fat is extremely important as it stabilizes and strengthens the immune system which halts infections and is necessary to ensure the calcium we eat actually makes it into our bones. Oil is necessary for optimal body functions. However it has got to be a good high quality saturated fat. Best options available are pure butter (not margarine), extra virgin olive oil and virgin coconut oil. Coconut oil is natural, tropical oil that is extracted in a straight forward manner from coconuts simply by applying pressure. Moreover it is loaded with medium-chain saturated fatty acids (MCTs). MCT is a distinct type of fatty acid that our body has a difficult time storing. This means MCTs are more readily available for energy while burning body fat at the same time. Coconut oil contains full of a mono-glyceride called lauric acid which is naturally antimicrobial and antibacterial. Coconut oil is known to aid in improving ailments such as low thyroid function, diabetes, bacterial infections, obesity, asthma, skin disorders, hair loss and a various health issues. Many people have had great success eating it daily to support sustain and maintain weight loss (1-2 Tbsp/day, ideally in the morning does wonders). In some instances, it showed that coconut oil consumption actually helped people lose belly fat and raise protective HDL cholesterol levels. Therefore "oily" is not such a bad thing as perceived. It's just that we need to consume the right oil.

Ghee is a Definitely a Better Option

Ghee is originated from India and is known to be India's heritage and a therapeutic one that is. Ghee is made by the simplest method. Therefore, it is far from being processed food. The consistency of ghee is easy to consume. The numerous health benefits of ghee are very much described only in Naturopathy. From good looks to sharp brains, from overcoming constipation to spiritual growth and evolution, ghee is celebrated in Naturopathy for many reasons – gross to subtle, small and big.

The Health benefits of Ghee

Great skin, lubricated joints, stronger immune functions, better memory, heart health, fertility, anti-carcinogenic and everything in between. The super crucial attribute these days is for assimilation of Vitamin D, because Vitamin D deficiency is the rich man's new disease.

How much Ghee a day? We can have Ghee as much as we want, as much as is required to bring about the best texture, flavor, aroma and taste of the food we are preparing. (No, its NOT cholesterol)

What type of ghee are we to take? Naturopathy prefers the homemade ghee that follows all the protocol and tops the list – being distilled, or purified from milk to curd, curd to butter, and churned and then heated. Its best if the milk is from grass fed cow, the one that walks around and grazes on nutritious grass. Not the foreign, black, brown and white polka dot cows that are fed with corn and hormones and kept in-doors. The order should be, grass fed cows, followed by buffalos and the last option is QBB brand (the closest to original ghee).

The weight watchers, the health conscious who worry about cardiovascular diseases and most of all, the ones who dread "oily" food would be skeptical when it comes to ghee. We confuse ghee with other saturated fat. At one time, we believed that fat was no good at all and kept away from it as much as possible. Then, we leant that not all fat is bad. It is right to avoid saturated fat that comes in cookies, biscuits and cereals, but is also important to understand that the saturated fat in ghee is unlike in nature when compared to the one that is found in packaged or processed food. Ghee has a very distinctive carbon atom structure, which is much tinier in molecular structure than the usual and commonly found and rightfully feared saturated fat. It is this distinctive carbon atom chain that gives ghee all its magical properties and beneficial effects when administered with Naturopathy therapies. This basic chemistry is overlooked due to a consequence of partial information.

Ghee is versatile fat by nature. It compliments any type of meal and enhances its flavor. It can be taken hot, cold or warm. A Naturopathy diet has ghee in all its preparations. According to Framingham and Nurses studies, animal fat has little or no association with heart disease risks and it should be the major dietary calorie source. This saturated animal fat has been around and in human evolution and Naturopathy since existence. In Naturopathy, it promotes efficient fat metabolism and stable energy levels. No studies have directly pointed saturated fat to heart diseases. Major risk factor for heart disease however, is actually metabolic syndrome, driven by excess polyunsaturated fatty acids, insufficient Omega 3s, high carbohydrate, excess insulin and overly stressful lifestyle.

Hydrogenated oil (Trans-fat) is to be avoided completely

Hydrogenated oil (Trans-fats) is unsaturated fats which are abnormal in nature and this oil can also be created artificially. In its natural state hydrogenated oil is considered quite healthy. If we're really concerned about our health and wish to stay healthy, then we need to be very concerned about what we're putting into our body. We need to be consciously aware of what we eat.

Hydrogenated oil or Trans-fat has its own special place in almost all food labels these days. A lot of these foods literally have a special place in our hearts too. We all grew up eating hydrogenated oil or Trans-fat without even knowing it was there. Trans-fat became favored by consumers and food manufacturers because it acts as a remarkable preservative, giving foods an extended shelf life. It also gives food a more tempting taste, attractive color and admirable texture.

We need to avoid popular fast foods, hawker's foods, catered luncheons, cakes, cookies, biscuits and many other known junk foods as all these food are definitely prepared using hydrogenated oil. We need to understand, realize and consciously be aware that more than 6000 chemicals are added to our foods today. Most of these chemicals have negative side effects and quite a number of these compounds are known health destroyers. All processed chemicals that are used in foods have serious detrimental effects on human health and energy levels on the long run. These chemicals have somehow crept into our diet in a subtle manner. Our modern day diet is full of these chemicals and we consume it on a daily basis without even realizing it. The worst of its kind is hydrogenated and partially hydrogenated oils and these oils champion the lists of chemical foods.

To understand this, let's evaluate hydrogenated oils and see what its properties truly are and why it's so unbelievably bad for us. Although hydrogenated oils are oils that are quite healthy in their original state, they are instantly turned into harmful toxins through the extensive manufacturing processes it undergoes. Capitalizing Manufacturers take these naturally healthy oils and heat it for up to about a thousand degrees under several different conditions of high pressure. They then inject a catalyst into the oil for several hours. (Catalyst is a substance that increases the rate of a chemical reaction without itself undergoing any permanent chemical change). Catalyst is actually a piece of metal such as platinum, nickel or even aluminum. This metal bubbles up into the oil changing the molecular structure of the oil and increasing in density and rearranging its molecules so that instead of a liquid at room temperature we now have either semi-solid or solid oil. This fabricates either partially hydrogenated or fully hydrogenated oils.

The molecules in this new by-product are now closer to cellulose or fine plastic particles rather than to oil. In actual fact hydrogenated oil is only one molecule away from being the purest form of premature plastic. Picture what happens to us when we eat anything containing this material? After going through all the processing stages, the oil becomes thicker and more viscous (dense). We can just imagine what happens to our blood when we carelessly consume this oil. Just like the oil, our blood too becomes thicker with high viscosity right along with the hydrogenated oil we consume. Our heart is burdened and now has to work so much harder to pump blood throughout our entire system. This is one of the prime reasons why consuming hydrogenated oils contributes and gradually leads to high blood pressure.

Our thickened blood with all its tiny bits of gluey particles flowing with it in our system, can easily lodge in the arteries and build up the arterial plaque. It doesn't take too much time as we may think for this to occur. Some studies have shown that negative health effects of eating processed foods occurs within only minutes of consuming such foods depending on the vulnerable state of our body.

Besides contributing to high cholesterol, hydrogenated oils are actually known to be abrasive to the internal walls of the arteries. This is because of the nickel that is often used in the manufacturing process. This causes the body (liver) to then produce more cholesterol to heal the walls of the arteries. This is one reason that the plaque builds up rapidly on the arterial walls. As the walls are continually scarred, this slowly narrows the opening for blood to flow through making the heart work much harder, exerting it and placing a great strain on our heart's pumping. This thicker blood now has a harder time pumping through the arteries and also up to our brain. As this continues the micro circulation of blood through our brain slows down and eventually wears our heart out too.

Hydrogenated oils became popular simply because they are superb as preservatives. Almost all the bio-chemical activity in the oil is neutralized during the process of hydrogenating. Since, this hydrogenated oil is only one molecule away from premature plastic particles and plastic does not breakdown at all, it can last in or body for a lifetime.

If un-hydrogenated oils were put into foods, it would go stale very quickly. This would increase the cost for the mass manufacturers. This is why even a small food outlet cannot afford to use natural oils. Their food will go stale very fast and losses will be incurred. Food will rot quicker at room temperature if prepared with natural oils simply because of the consistent enzymatic activity occurring in them. Any food that does not go bad in 8 hours at room temperature is regarded as "dead" food and is inappropriate for consumption.

Our food has enzymes and consistent enzymatic activity taking place in it. It is a known fact that the faster a particular food goes bad, the healthier it usually is. When we consume healthy enzymatic food, it also means that the enzymatic activity within our own body will be healthier as well. Food is basically meant to be auto-digested by our system. So eating foods high in natural enzymes such as fresh vegetables, fruits and other raw foods directly translates to less stress on our own digestive system. The more enzyme dead food we consume, the more our own body has to create and use up its own food enzymes during digestion. An overburdened pancreas is actually one of the major causes of Type II diabetes which is basically pancreatic failure.

Digestion of hydrogenated oil takes a massive amount of enzymes and energy from the system. Even with optimum state of energy, our body never really succeeds in complete assimilation of hydrogenated oil because this material is not natural and it's a substance that the body is not designed to absorb. Such invasion of foreign substances often cause false immune response which place a great strain on the immune system and decreases overall immunity.

As the body secretes more enzymes (digestive acids) in the stomach to try and digest this man made oil, the internal stomach digestive fire (temperature) rises. This is another way that these unhealthy oils can lead to diseases. The amount of heat required to break down plastic can go up to thousands of degrees. Therefore, with all the intelligence, our body is often only partially successful at breaking down and digesting hydrogenated oils.

The walls of our cells are normally made up of healthy oils such as Omega-3 and Omega-6 fats, also known as essential fatty acids (EFA's) found in fish oils and grass fed animal meats. The walls of our cells are the cell's shielding (defense) mechanism, so it's crucial that they have sufficient EFA's in the cell wall. It is the EFA that allows nutrients to be absorbed and waste matter to be flushed out of the cell while keeping foreign invaders and disease causing micro-organisms out.

When hydrogenated oil reaches the cells, the cells try to digest, absorb and transform the hydrogenated oil into the actual configuration of the cell wall. When there are not enough essential fatty acids, the cells are forced to use this detrimental hydrogenated oil into its cellular matrix to fulfill the difference. What's worse is that this new cell wall which is now made up of hydrogenated oils is almost ineffective and this weakens the very function of the cell wall.

The presence of sticky substances from hydrogenated oils in the cell walls actually blocks valuable nutrients from entering the cell and at the same time allowing toxic pathogens, microbes and viruses to pass through. It also prevents toxic waste material from getting out of the cell. When the much needed nutrients are kept out of the cell and the waste matter that is to be expelled is now trapped in the cell, the cell mutates or dies which can lead to cancer, tumors or other serious health deficiencies.

How do we avoid hydrogenated Oils?

To avoid hydrogenated oils, we need to keep most of our foods in and as close to its natural state as possible. This means more fruits and vegetables when eating out. All food outlets including star restaurants use hydrogenated oils in the food preparation and cooking due to its cost effectiveness. The more the real foods we eat from nature, the lesser the damage to our body. Packaged and processed foods must be avoided totally. It's the canned, packaged and processed foods that are most likely to be made with hydrogenated oils because there is a need for shelf life to be increased.

This really means we have to convert and make a drastic change in the way that we think about food and what we classify as food. Perfect foods are those that are directly from nature, in its natural pristine state, and not those that come out of a factory, a can or a box. We can't rely on the government or any other source to tell us what is ok to put into our body or the body of our loved ones.

We need to become an absolutely smart label reader and check everything we buy, be it packaged and processed. We especially need to be certain that hydrogenated oils are not listed as ingredients, even on packages that have the word "organic" on the pack. Just because a package has the word organic on the label doesn't mean that it's necessarily a healthy food. Packaged and processed foods with "organic" on the box would really be considered "less damaging" but not truly 100% healthy. Healthy food is food full of enzymes, phyto-nutrients, and life force with all its natural vitamins and minerals present. Enzymes are actually more important than any vitamins, minerals or other nutrients since all processes that occur in the body must have sufficient supplies of enzymes to do their job optimally. Foods that have had their enzymes destroyed are automatically classified as "dead foods" by Naturopathy.

Hydrogenated and partially hydrogenated oils are the worst ingredient in the modern food products today. This is a destructive man made oil that must be totally avoided. This is especially important if we're looking to recover from any form of illnesses or working towards an optimum state of health.

Word of caution: Stop eating out. Beware that eating out even in posh restaurants can pose just as great a health risk as packaged and processed foods do. Almost all restaurants use hydrogenated oils in all their food preparations. This is another reason that eating out often can have very negative health effects. The best solution is to prepare our own foods at home as often as we can and getting as far away as possible from processed food diet. This is the only way we know exactly what we're putting into our body and not surrendering it up to modern manufacturers of today's so called "foods" that have no concern at all for our health or well being. Note: Hydrogenated and partially hydrogenated oils are another name for Trans-Fatty Acids.

Our relationship with food

We have to understand and establish a great relationship with the food that we eat. Understanding the nutritional value, the right amount of food, the number of times we eat; keeping in mind the well known philosophy "everything in moderation" is a great way to support ourselves towards a healthy relationship with food.

Delving further into our psyche, we could ask ourselves these questions (we may even want to maintain a food journal, to write out how, why, when, and what we feel when eating or not eating particular foods — to really pinpoint our eating pattern):

- Do we have sufficient energy throughout the day to carry out our daily activities?
- How content are we, for the most part, with our relationships?
- Do we miss social functions or excitedly look forward to these occasions due to our "plain" eating habits?
- Do we really consider ourselves health conscious? Or, would "health anxious" be a more suitable description?

Intervals between Meals

The mind hates routine but the body adores it. The mind loves freedom but the body loves stability. Digestion is demanding on resources. The body schedules eating times to make sure resources are available.

Do Not Eat Until at Least Four Hours after a Meal

The stomach processes food for approximately Four hours while slowly releasing it into the duodenum. Wait until the stomach is empty. Do not eat anything for four hours after eating a complete meal. Avoid water immediately after meals.

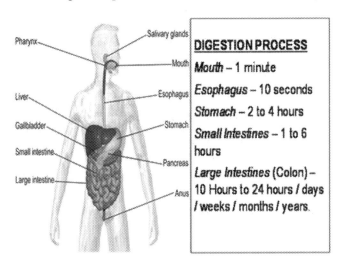

DIGESTION PROCESS

Mouth – 1 minute

Esophagus – 10 seconds

Stomach – 2 to 4 hours

Small Intestines – 1 to 6 hours

Large Intestines (Colon) – 10 Hours to 24 hours / days / weeks / months / years.

Preparing the Stomach and Taste Buds

Bitter, pungent, salty and sour tastes help kick start digestion. Bitter neem, bitter gourd or mint stimulates peristalsis. While Europeans stimulate digestion with alcoholic aperitifs, Naturopathy recommends lime for sour taste. A ginger, lime, salt appetizer refreshes the taste buds, stimulates saliva, and brings blood flow to the digestive tract.

Introduction to Naturopathy Diet

Naturopathy believes that health, wealth, and happiness come from harmonic balance with nature. The first and most important tool for this harmonic balance is a good diet. Good diet is the foundation for emotional and physical health. Naturopathy has a very sophisticated knowledge of the effects of food and the manner in which we consume it. The practice of Naturopathy began in ancient India over 9,000 years ago. Although we have this practice from ancient times, we are still very much at a lost when it comes to proper diet. There can never be a standard diet plan that everyone can follow. No two blades of grass look the same. No two birds of a feather look alike. No two cows from the same flock look alike. Similarly we human too are never the same where size, activity level, energy level, looks, thinking pattern, livelihood and lifestyle differs. We may belong to the same family but we differ in many ways. Therefore diet too differs. We need to identify and understand our ideal diet. This is possible only if we seriously want optimum benefits from eating and start paying attention to what we eat.

Guideline to determine our Constitution

To determine our constitution it is best to fill out the chart hereafter twice. First base our choices on what is most consistent over a long period of our life, then fill it out a second time responding on how we had been feeling more recently. Sometimes, it helps to have a friend ask us the questions and fill in the chart for us, as they may have insight and impartiality to offer. After finishing the chart each time, add up the number of marks under vata, pitta and kapha. This will help us discover our ratio of constitution. Most of us will have one predominant constitution and some will have two equal constitutions and some will even have all three in equal proportions. For instance, if our first chart shows more pitta than our second, we will want to follow a pitta soothing regimen to try and bring back balance between the two states of condition. If both readings seem about the same, then we would choose the regimen of our strongest constitution.

Observations	V	P	K	VATA	PITTA	KAPHA
Body size				Slim	Medium	Large
Body weight				Low	Medium	Overweight
Chin				Thin, angular	Tapering	Rounded, double
Cheeks				Wrinkled, sunken	Smooth, Flat	Rounded, Plump
Eyes				Small, sunken, dry active, black, brown, nervous	Sharp, bright, grey, green, yellow/red, sensitive to light	Big, beautiful, blue, calm, loving
Nose				Uneven shape, deviated, septum	Long, pointed, red nose tip	Short rounded, button nose
Lips				Dry, cracked, black/brown, tinge	Red, inflamed, yellowish	Smooth, oily, pale, whitish

Teeth				Stick out, big, roomy, thin gums	Medium, soft, tender gums	Healthy, white strong gums
Skin				Thin, dry, cold, rough, dark	Smooth, oily, warm, rosy	Thick, oily, cool, white, pale
Hair				Dry, brown, black, knotted, brittle, scarce	Straight, oily, blonde, grey, red, bald	Thick, curly, oily, wavy, luxuriant
Nails				Dry, rough, brittle, break easily	Sharp, flexible, pink, lustrous	Thick, oily, smooth, polished
Neck				Thin, Tall	Medium	Big, folded
Chest				Flat, sunken	Moderate	Expanded, round
Belly				Thin, flat, sunken	Moderate	Big, pot bellied
Belly Button				Small, irregular, herniated	Oval, superficial	Big, Deep, Round, Stretched
Hips				Slender, thin	Moderate	Heavy, Big
Joints				Cold, cracking	Moderate	Large, lubricated
Appetite				Irregular, scanty	Strong, unbearable	Slow but steady
Digestion				Irregular, forms gas	Quick, causes burning	Prolonged, forms mucous
Taste				Sweet, sour, salty	Sweet, bitter, astringent	Bitter, pungent, astringent
Thirst				Changeable	Surplus	Sparse
Elimination				Constipation	Loose	Thick, oily, sluggish
Physical activity				Hyperactive	Moderate	Slow
Mental Activity				Hyperactive	Moderate	Dull, slow
Emotions				Anxiety, fear, uncertainty	Anger, hate, jealousy	Calm, greedy, attachment
Faith				Variables	Extremist	Consistent
Intellect				Quick but faulty response	Accurate response	Slow, exact
Recollection				Recent good, remote poor	Distinct	Slow and sustained
Dreams				Quick, active, many, fearful	Fiery, war, violence	Lakes, snow, romantic

Sleep				Scanty, broken-up, sleeplessness	Little but sound	Deep, prolonged
Speech				Rapid, unclear	Sharp, penetrating	Slow, monotonous
Financial				Poor, spends on trifles	Spends money on luxuries	Rich, good money preserver
Total						

The Balance in a Diet

- When we are preparing our assortment of foods for a meal, there is a need to look at a particular category of the foods and select more foods in the alkaline category.

- This alkaline food chart given hereafter is only accurate for certain state of the foods. For example, cooked lettuce has a different pH value compared to a boiled lettuce or raw lettuce.

- The food chart is based on a number of acid alkaline food charts, research, information from nutritionists, and doctors. If we find a conflict with other alkaline food charts, sign up for our newsletters at www.tammmf.org and you'll discover the alkaline principles behind these differences.

- This alkaline food chart is based on the **"residue** "of the foods after it has been digested in the stomach. This is why we will find that lemon is alkaline and not acidic.

Acidic and Alkaline Food

ACIDIC FRUIT & ALKALINE FRUIT

Mildly Acidic	Alkaline	Alkaline	Alkaline	Highly Alkaline
Blueberry	Acai berry	Red Apple	Apricot	Avacado
Sweet Cherry	Banana	Black Current	Black Berries	Fresh Figs
Canned Tomatoes	Cantaloupe	Tart Cherry	Coconut	Goji Berries
Canned Fruits	Cranberry	Dates	Dragon Fruit	Kiwi
Coctails	Dried Figs	Dried Figs	Goose Berries	Lemons
Moctails	Grapefruit	Grapes	Italian Plum	Lime
Preserved Fruit	China Oranges	Mango	Nectarine	Star Fruit
Dried Fruits	Orange	Papaya	Peach	Green Apple
	Pear	Pineapple	Pomegranate	Watermelon
	Raspberry	Red Current	Rose Hip	Persimmon
	Strawberry	Tangerine	Tomato	
	Tangerine	Watermelon	Yellow Plum	

GRAINS

Acidic	Mildly Acidic	Mildly Acidic	Alkaline	Highly Alkaline
White Rice	Barley	Basmati Rice	Wild Rice	
Corn	Brown Rice	Kamut	Barley Grass	
Pasta	Oats	Spelt	Buckwheat	
Wheat			Quinoa	

LEGUMES

Acidic	Mildly Acidic	Mildly Alkaline	Mildly Alkaline	Alkaline
Black Bean	Chickpeas	Lenthils	Lima Beans	Green Beans
Kidney Beans		Mung Beans	Navy Beans	Soy Lecithin
		Pinto Beans	Red Beans	Sprouted Beans
		Soy Beans	White Beans	

VEGETABLES

Acidic	Mildly Alkaline	Alkaline	Alkaline	Highly Alkaline
Canned Vegetable	Watercress	Cilantro	Bok Choy	Parsley
Cooked Vegetable	Bell Peppers	Brussels Sprouts	Cabbage	Broccoli
Frozen Vegetables	Cauliflower	Cayenne Pepper	Celery	Cucumber
Pickled Vegetables	Chives	Spinach	Tomato (raw)	Wheat Grass
Sour cabbage	Lettuce	Endive(Fresh)	Garlic	Soy Sprouts
	Onion	Lettuce	Mustard Green	Spring Onion
	Parsnips	Oregano	Peppers	Mint
	Peas (Fresh)	Pumpkins	Red Cabbage	All Sprouted seeds
	Squash		Sea Vegetable	Celery

ROOTS

Mildly Alkaline	Mildly Alkaline	Mildly Alkaline	Alkaline	Highly Alkaline
Carrot	Kohlrabi	Potato	Ginseng	Ginger
Rutabaga	Sweet Potato	Turnip	Beetroot	Jicama (Sengkuang)
White Raddish	Yams	Tapioca	Red Radish	Black Radish

NUTS & SEEDS

Acidic	Mildly Acidic	Mildly Alkaline	Mildly Alkaline	Mildly Alkaline
Peanut Butter	Brazil Nuts	Almonds	Almond Butter raw)	Pine Nuts (raw)
Peanuts	Cashew Nuts	Caraway Seeds	Cumin Seeds	Fennel Seeds
Pistachios	Hazelnuts	Sesame Seeds	Flax Seeds	Pumpkin Seeds
Pecans	Macadamia Nuts	Sunflower Seeds		
Chestnuts	Nutmeg			
Wheat Kernel	Walnuts			

SWEETS & SWEETENERS

Highly Acidic	Acidic	Mildly Acidic	Mildly Alkaline	Alkaline
Artificial Sweeteners	Brown Rice Syrup	Agave Nectar	Barley Malt Syrup	Black Molasses
Beet Sugar	Chocolate	Honey	Maple Syrup	Stevia
Corn Syrup	Sugar Cane	Jam	Raw Sugar	Palm Sugar
Sugar (white)	Saccharine			

FROM THE BAKERY

Acidic	Acidic	Mildly Acidic	Mildly Acidic	Mildly Acidic
Sourdough Bread	White Bread	White Biscuits	Whole Meal Bread	Spelt Bread
Corn Tortillas	Pancakes	Rye Bread	Sprouted Bread	Wheat Bread
Cakes	Fruit Cake	Cookies	Biscuits	Savory Biscuits

FATS & OIL

Mildly Acidic	Acidic	Alkaline	Mildly Alkaline	Mildly Alkaline
Canola Oil	Peanut Oil	Ghee	Borage Oil	Coconut Oil
Cod Liver Oil	Vegetable Oil	Flax Seed Oil	Flax Seed Oil	Marine Lipids
Sunflower Oil	Hydrogenated Oil	Gingerly oil	Sesame Oil	Udo's Oil
Corn Oil		Any Seed Oil	Avocado Oil	Evening Primrose
Margarine			Olive Oil	Butter

MEAT, POULTRY & FISH

Highly Acidic	Highly Acidic	Acidic	Acidic	Acidic
Bacon	Beef	Carp	Chicken	Clams
Buffalo	Canned Sardines	Cod	Duck	Fresh Water Fish
Canned Tuna	Lamb	Liver	Lobster	Mussels
Organ Meat	Pork	Ocean Fish	Oyster	Tuna
Sausage	Turkey	Rabbit	Scallops	Salmon
Veal	Venison	Sardines	Shellfish	Shrimp

BEVERAGES & DRINKS

Acidic	Highly Acidic	Acidic	Acidic	Alkaline
Beer	Carbonated Drinks	Sweetened Juice	Sparkling Water	Natural Fruit Juice
Liquor	'Teh Tarik'	Black Tea	Wine	Tea (Herbal, Green)
Chocolate Drink	Condensed Milk	Coffee	Soda/Pop	Water (Fiji, Evian)

MISCELLANEOUS

Highly Acidic	Acidic	Mildly Acidic	Mildly Alkaline	Alkaline
Candy	Canned Food	Whey Protein	Apple Cider Vinegar	Baking Soda
Chips	All Cereals	Mushrooms	Bee Pollen	Goats Milk
Cigarettes	Micro waved Food	Rice Milk	Royal Jelly	Almond Milk
Drugs	Miso	Soy Milk	Tempeh	Sea Salt
Pizza	Popcorn	Soy Protein Powder	Tofu	Seaweed
Anything Refined	Ketchup	Yogurt		
Junk Food	Mustard			
Anything Preserved	Soy Sauce			

Bookmark this guide and come back to this page whenever there's a need. **Share this page with our friends in Facebook via TA MARIANTHONY MERCY MISSION FOUNDATION. Take it** with us wherever we go and show it to our friends and family and discuss this chart till we become an expert at understanding food and its relationship with us.

The Actual Functions of Food

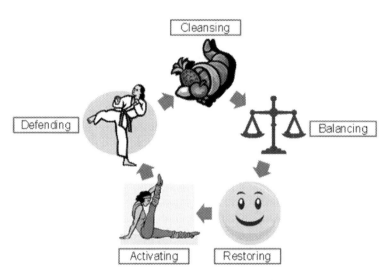

Cleansing -   Process of removing toxins from the body to keep us healthy

Balancing -   Process of maintaining sufficient nutrients in the body.

Restoring -   Process of regulating our body's nutritional needs.

Activating -   Process of replenishing the nutritional level of the organs to restore and revitalize cells and body functions.

Defending -   Process of defending against diseases.

Optimum Benefits From Foods

- Eating a diet rich in alkaline foods can help ensure maximum benefit of negative ion exposure, while reducing the harmful effects of positive ions. Vegetables and fruits that are alkaline (containing a higher pH), reduce the acidification of the blood. Similarly, foods that are acidic can reduce the amount of negative ions found in the body and should be avoided.

3 Vital Functions of – VE IONS

CLEANSING	Cleanses the entire system, Assists in purifying blood, eliminates bacteria, Disinfect and detoxification
BALANCING	Balances body acid-alkaline Level, boosts the function of the body system
NOURISHING	Assists in red blood cell Generation, enhances oxidation process and stimulates cell regeneration

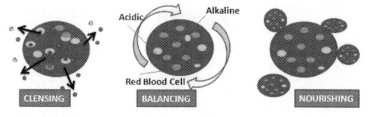

Comparing -ve ions & +ve ions

	Effects of –ve ions	Effects of +ve ions
Blood vessels	Expand	Contracts
Blood pressure	Normal	Rises
Blood Ph	Alkaline	Acidic
Bones	Strong	Weak
Urination	Good	Disorder
Breathing	Normal	Disorder
Pulse	Normal	Fast
Heart	Normal	Disorder
Fatigue	Recovers fast	Persistent
Nervous system	Stable	Panic Attacks

Effects of Negative Ions on our Body

- Negative ions treatments are used in Naturopathy to treat depression, migraines and asthma. The body's energy system is fundamentally electromagnetic in nature. Although there is not yet sound scientific proof, some scientists suggest that a negatively-charged environment stimulates blood circulation and increases the blood flow of oxygenated blood to all of the cells throughout the body. Sometimes even to relieve pain to a certain extent.

Negative ions?

While positive ions are also known as the harmful free radicals that are emitted from things such as microwaves and toxic chemicals, Naturopathy believes negative ions actually have a healing effect on the body. Unlike positive ions which lack an electron, negative ions are ion molecules of oxygen in the air with an extra electron. Negative ions are typically found in higher concentrations around mountains, meadows, waterfalls, beaches, and forests. A holiday by the beach is very relaxing because of negative ions. We can close our eyes and absorb the calmness and serenity at a waterfall simply because we inhale the negative ions that immediately relaxes and energizes our mind. Urban areas such as office buildings, bus terminals, shopping complexes, wet markets and other congested areas have much lower levels of negative ions that makes us tired, drained and worn out.

Naturopathy Characteristics of Food

Understanding the characteristics of food is the most important aspect of a Naturopathy diet. Naturopathy is about how comfortable we feel after we eat. To know naturopathy, we have to relate to the characteristics of the food we eat. The first eight characteristics are heavy and light, sharp and dull, hot and cold, oily and dry. For example bread is heavy but salads are light. Black pepper is sharp but cheese is dull. Chilies are hot but cucumbers are cool. Butter is oily but popcorn is dry. We need to select food that is most beneficial to us.

Naturopathy groups all diseases into three general categories called Vatha, Pitha and Kapha. This simply means small, medium and large. These categories describe three basic patterns of how we use energy. Vatha spends energy. Pittha manages it. Kapha stores it. It also predicts how the body responds to change. For example, Kapha and Vatha rise in response to cold temperature. Pittha rises in response to hot temperature.

Our Taste Buds

In Naturopathy, nutrition is based on six taste buds contrary to the West that identifies only four tastes. Bitter is light and drying. Astringent is tightening and drying. Pungent is sharp and dry. Salty taste is liquefying and hot. Sour is hot, liquefying, and heavy. Sweet taste is heavy, gooey, and cold. In Naturopathy, every season has a different taste and our diet needs to be in harmony with the seasons as well.

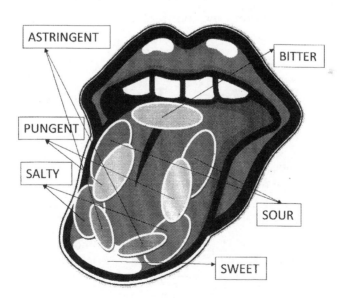

Digestion

Good circulation, good digestion and well nourished tissues are three cornerstones of good health. By the magic of digestion, when we eat an apple it becomes a part of our body. Whether the apple is hot or cold, acidic or basic, sugary or bitter, the body still has to transform the qualities of the apple into the qualities of a human being. Everything we eat becomes us. Digestion takes to work in assimilation of the apple completely. Our body's intelligence will signal us when there is indigestion. Some signs of indigestion include gas, burping, acid reflux, diarrhea and constipation.

Evolution & Taste Buds

Taste buds evolved because they are important for maintaining our health. Our taste buds are vital to our existence. Move a farm animal 1000 km away from its home ground and within days it will identify all the wild edible plants in the surroundings. Taste buds have helped our ancestors survive in the wild and our tongue is a precise amazing laboratory for our health. Naturopathy identifies six tastes: sweet, sour, salty, pungent, bitter, and astringent.

Cravings & Creation

Taste is desire and appreciating and understanding good taste is an art. As our tastes change our food choices change. Taste is the mother of creation because food creates the body. Similarly the sexual organs transform desire and choice into creation and fertility. This is why taste and sex are linked in Naturopathy. Tastes are not only on our tongue but also in the choices of our clothing. We often decorate our homes according to our taste. In the law of attraction, our tastes and lifestyle determines and changes who and what kind of people and energy we attract.

Tastes & Emotions

Every human being is made up of emotions. Emotions are in the mind but we express them with our mouth. A smile means we are happy. Tastes are the emotions of the body and are also located in the mouth. Emotions and tastes can change quickly and unpredictably. An orange that tastes sweet yesterday may taste sour today. Every food has a 'taste personality' which takes some time to figure out. Generally eating a certain type of food daily for three weeks will help us discover the personality of the food in our body.

Tastes & Health

Every taste is associated with a physical and emotional response. Sweet taste causes physical satisfaction and attraction whereas bitter taste causes discomfort and aversion. Knowledge of taste brings awareness to our food cravings. A balanced Naturopathy diet includes all of the six tastes in every meal but each individual should adjust the quantity of the tastes for his or her body. For example, kapha should use less sweet taste. Vata and Pitta use more sweet taste. An organism can have an excess or deficiency of taste which can be detected by a Dieter who practices Naturopathy way of eating.

Cravings for Food

Tastes are not in the food but on the tongue. One of the first signs of illness is altered taste. Altered taste leads to poor food choices and cravings. When taste buds are altered we recommend a through cleansing of our body. This cleansing will remove excess negativities from the body.

Cravings are our body's best attempt to heal itself. For example excess kapha causes circulation to stagnate and low energy. Then kapha craves sweets for a quick 'pick-me-up'. Sweet cravings might have been appropriate for our ancestors in the wilderness but there were no ice-cream cones in the forest! In modern society however indulging in ice cream only causes more kapha stagnation and cravings.

Our Cravings Interpreted

OUR CRAVINGS	WHAT WE NEED	WHAT WE NEED TO EAT INSTEAD
Chocolate	Magnesium	Nuts, Seeds, Vegetables, Fruits
Sugary Foods	Chromium	A few pieces of Chicken, Grapes, Cheddar Cheese, Broccoli
	Carbon	Any fresh Fruit
	Phosphorous	Chicken, beef, fatty fish, eggs, dairy, nuts, raw vegetable, grains
	Sulphur	Cranberries, cabbage, cauliflower
	Tryptophan	Cheese, raisins, sweet potatoes, Spinach
Bread, Rice, Pasta & Other Carbohydrates	Nitrogen	High protein foods, meat, fatty fish, nuts, beans, sago, chia seeds
Oily foods	Calcium	Organic milk, cheese, green leafy vegetable
Salty Food	Silicon	Cashews, nuts, seeds

Sacred Craving

Cravings are different from hunger. Cravings are caused by nutrient deficiencies. All cravings come from unhealthy or deficient organs. By understanding taste and the nature of the deficiency we can understand the root of our cravings. When health and desire are one our cravings become sacred.

Sweet Food

Sweet tasting food includes nourishing foods like carbohydrates, fats and proteins. Sweet taste means good tasting but not necessarily sugary. Before refined sugars, bread tasted naturally sweet. Sweet taste is life giving. It builds vigor, meaning it nourishes the sap or blood plasma of the body.

Sweet tasting food is rare in nature and desirable. We need sweet tasting food to survive. But man being man, monopolized this need and produced refined sugar. After this agricultural revolution, sweet tasting food became abundant. It dominates the modern grocery stores these days.

Sweet and Circulation

Excess use of sweet tasting food, especially refined grains and refined sugars, thickens blood plasma. Thick, sticky blood plasma bogs circulation causing stagnation and high blood pressure. Poor circulation also causes water retention resulting in swelling in the hands and feet.

Sweet and Skin

When circulation is excessively boggy, metabolic byproducts (cellular poop) get trapped in the lymphatic system causing inflammation. To see this effect more clearly, make a thumbprint on our arm. A white thumbprint surrounded by red skin could mean the lymphatic system is stagnant and inflamed. Note: This effect is usually prominent on the arms and legs.

Sweet, Lungs & the Thyroid

Healthy lungs depend on good circulation to keep them hollow. Otherwise, the lungs fill up with mucous and water. Excess sweet tasting food causes mucous buildup in the lungs and back of throat. Boggy circulation and a thick layer of mucous covering the lungs reduce circulation of oxygen (prana). The thyroid compensates by lowering metabolism. Many people have low thyroid activity. Symptoms of low thyroid include being overweight, cold body temperature, dry skin, and constipation.

Sweet and the Kidneys

Dense, gooey, sticky blood plasma causes water retention in the kidneys and may lead to edema. While kapha types are prone to this and should discourage water retention, dry vata types can use the sweet taste to help retain fluids.

Naturopathy Classifications for Sweet

Sweet taste is cooling, heavy, oily, and sticky. It brings softness and stability. Sweet taste coats the tongue and throat. It facilitates elimination of bowels. It is beneficial to children, during old age, and in debilitated persons. Sweet taste alleviates thirst, pacifies pitta and vata, and nourishes the mind. Sweet taste helps in wound healing as long as the wound is not infected. Therefore, a healthy balance of sweet tasting food is vital for a Naturopathic diet.

Remedies for Excess Sweet

Bitter food like Kale, Bitter gourd, green leafy vegetable and Moringa directly opposes sweet taste. They are drying to our system, regulate blood sugar levels, reduce cholesterol, and aids in thinning the blood. Pungent taste, including black pepper and ginger stimulates circulation and heat that balances body temperature.

Sour Food

When something spoils or goes rotten, it becomes sour. Sour taste in Naturopathy generally refers to fermented foods as in, "the milk has gone sour", or any other acidic food. Sour food includes curd, yogurt, wine, beer, miso, tauchu and pickles. Generally these sour foods are believed to weaken the blood. Thank heavens, nature provides us with healthy sour food as well which includes acidic fruit like citrus, gooseberries, bilimbi, star fruit and sub-acidic fruits like peaches, apples, mangoes etc.

Sour and Secretions

Sour pacifies vata. Sours are actually secretagogues. A secretagogue is a substance that causes another substance to be secreted. They dampen and stimulate a dry palate, stimulating secretions throughout the GI tract. Salivary secretions improve taste. Gastric secretions in the stomach improve digestion. Moistening the colon facilitates smoother, looser and easier bowel movements.

Sour Spoils the Blood

The thought of something sour immediately accumulates saliva in our mouth. This is why we always add a tiny bit of pickle, sour cream, curd or yogurt in our meal. But it must be limited to only a spoonful as sour ferments are hot and spoil the blood, aggravating Pitta. All fermented foods are pre-digested by bacterium, therefore they are easily absorbed through the GI tract. Very small amount of sours help increase the blood circulation in our gut. In Chinese traditional medication, they "generate" the liver. Pre-digestion means, the fermented food contain metabolic by-products or "bacteria excrement." It is the bioavailability of nutrients, combined with agitated metabolic by-products, that stimulates metabolism in all tissues, and sparks the liver and causes the blood to weaken. Sour food increases limpness of tissues and decreases strength of the sense organs. Our sense organs are;

Eyes	-----------------------	Sight
Ears	-----------------------	Hearing
Tongue	-----------------------	Taste
Nose	-----------------------	Smell
Skin	-----------------------	Touch

Sour Heightens Desire

People tend to love wine because it instantly dilates blood vessels and focuses the mind. It triggers our desires, which are mostly sexual. These desires, most of time, cannot be fulfilled as our body does not cooperate with the mind. Our mind becomes slower than the body. When our desires aren't fulfilled it could lead to disappointment ('sour grapes') as in Aesop's fable, "The Fox and the Grapes." Grapes are supposed to be sweet. We do not like eating grapes that have turned sour. In sour grapes, it means our heart dismisses or rejects that which is desired.

Sour Fruits

Sour fruits are more sentient than ferments. They refresh and cleanse the palate. Imagine a lemon sorbet between courses at a fine French restaurant. Basically a sour fruit intensifies the digestion heat but not the blood. There are two categories for sour fruits - acidic and mildly-acidic. Acidic fruits include citrus fruits like lemons, limes, and oranges. Mildly-acidic fruits include peaches, mangoes, grapes and pears. Mild-acidic fruits are the most sentient of all sours.

Sour and Chinese Medicine

According to Chinese medicinal practices, sour is construed as cooling because astringent taste is also included in sour taste. Pomegranates and cranberries are definite medicinal foods in Naturopathy because they are examples of sours with strong astringency. These sours react on dispersed energy bringing the spirit back to the heart. They are also worthy digestive tonics because; 1) sour food helps and supports digestion, 2) the cool aspect of sour food pacifies inflammation, and 3) astringency fixes and restores tone to tissues that swell due to pressure.

Salty Food

Salt and Flavor

A meal is never complete without salt. Salt gives a perfect touch to anything edible. Salt brings out the taste and flavor in food. And a flavor brings excitement and joy for life. It stimulates secretions improving digestion. Salt is a purgative that breaks down all hardened toxic masses in the digestive tract. Salt in excess extinguishes all other tastes and causes thirst. Therefore salt must be appropriate and balanced.

Salt and Liquefication

Salt induces water retention, increases blood pressure, and effectively counters dryness in vata. It cleanses the body by breaking up obstructions in all channels. Salt nourishes the nerve tissues. Salt dissolves kapha mucus in the lungs and sinuses.

Salt is used to induce vomiting in Naturopathy cleansing therapies. Patients are given to drink a quart of water with two teaspoons of salt to completely purge the GI tract.

Overuse of Salt

Naturopathy recommends limited use of only mineral salts. Refined salts should be avoided completely. Excess salt increases sagging and wrinkling of the skin causing lack of strength, vitality, or effectiveness. Salt pulls water into the intercellular space through osmosis, separating "fluid of life" from the tissues. It delays healing by causing secretions in wounds. In excess salt damages fluids, decreases libido, hardens muscles, damages bones, causes premature aging and ruins proper functions of the blood.

Salt, the Kidney, and Managing Fluids

The kidneys regulate the ocean of water in the body. Vata people with protein leaky kidneys actually benefit from anti-diuretics, like salt, licorice and vinegar. Anti-diuretics also help in reconditioning and restoring body fluids and acts against the diuretic effect of Vata type toxicity.

Many foods high in potassium, like potatoes, bananas and beans, are diuretics. Potassium and salt, work in an opposing manner in the body, both in fluid retention and on a cellular level. Salt aggravates kapha. Potassium appeases kapha.

Pungent

Pungent taste is present in spiced food and digestive enzymes. Pungent spices stimulate by irritating the lining of the digestive tract and other membranes. Made of fire element, pungent taste is sharp and concentrated, fast acting and intense, spreading quickly to all tissues. The forceful, constant contact of this pungent element penetrates burns, ulcerates, cuts and cauterizes. Therefore it is recommended that one suffering from such ailments, refrain from pungent food.

Types of Pungent Food

Black pepper and chilies are quintessential pungent. Hard liquor is pungent and burning. Sour taste, which increases secretions, is sharp but not pungent. In Naturopathy, pungent taste and the sharp quality of sour food is clumped together because they share many similarities.

Circulation & Immunity

Good circulation is stimulated by pungent food like ginger, black pepper and similar tasting pungent food. It improves our immunity and helps resolve minor ailments like sore throats.

The body flushes pungent irritants by thinning the blood, dilating blood vessels and increasing the heart rate. Pungent taste thus improves circulation. It also liquefies, softens, secretes and flushes out by breaking up and dissolving thick or hardened masses such as mucus. Pungent taste warms the liver which is responsible for blood thickening. Pungent taste expels excess vata, pitta, and kapha. Pungent taste stimulates courage and valor because blood flow is the movement of our digestive system's life force. REMEMBER! The immune system is in the blood.

Pungent & Kapha

Pungent taste is the best taste for kapha. Circulation increases heat, metabolism and our digestive strength. It burns off all kapha tissues creating lightness. It helps the body sweat, clearing and flushing all secretions. It breaks up and dries mucus in the GI tract and in the lungs. It wakes up the sleepy kapha mind and brings focus to mental activity.

Pungent & Vata

Vata should be careful with excess use of pungent taste. A small amount of pungent taste warms vata but pungent food should not be used to stimulate deficient organs. They increase Vata's already high metabolism which burns fluids in the vigorous aspects of drying out tissues. Instead, nourishment is the best way to rebuild organ strength for vata. Excess pungent taste over stimulates the vata mind. But ginger, pippali (tail pepper) and garlic are exceptions.

Pathological Pungency

Excess sharpness and pungent taste aggravates pitta and could lead to bleeding disorders, bruises, ulcers, inflammation and rash. After encouraging secretions, excess pungent taste leaves behind thirst and dryness as much as the hot sun dries the desert. Plain water is needed to balance of the state of dryness.

Treatment for Excess Pungent

Sweet, gooey foods coat and soothe excess pungency. Cooling demulcents like licorice ghee (Athimadura) and shatavari (Indian asparagus) are also indicated in Naturopathy for excessive pungent. Astringents like Amalaki (Nelli or Indian gooseberries) and arjuna (www.tammmf.org) too cools inflammation.

Astringent

Leafy greens, green bananas, grapes, rose apple (jambu air) and guavas are astringent. Astringent taste cleanses the mouth but causes difficulty swallowing. It is the astringent taste that makes an apple crunchy. It makes lentils and peeled potatoes stick to each other. Foods with astringent taste make the mouth feel rough or dry.

Astringent & Waste Products

Astringent taste causes a tightening of tissues obstructing lymphatic flow, movement of digestive toxins, metabolic waste and elimination of feces causing constipation. Astringent taste dries secretions and absorbs mucus (kapha).

Qualities of Astringent

Astringents are cooling and drying making them good for pitta inflammation on the skin and in the gastrointestinal tract (GI). However, one needs to be cautious if inflammation comes from dryness by itself (vata).

Astringent Taste & Emotions

Emotionally, an astringent taste helps someone to cool down and collect scattered thoughts. Astringent in the physical analog of fear causes the cells of the body to withdraw.

Astringent Herbs

Triphpala, Amalaki, Haritaki, Arjuna and Manjistha – for more info, logon to www.tammmf.org.

Bitter

Bitters and Digestion

Naturopathy suggests that a healthy gut will eliminate food six hours after eating it. The holy grail of six hour elimination exists today in indigenous societies with higher consumption of bitters but not for our society of refined flours and sugars.

The body perceives bitters as a poison and stimulates various organs for protection. In case of edible bitters, this has a beneficial, stimulating effect on digestion. Bitter food stimulates peristalsis, release of bile in the liver and gall bladder, and clears the blood of pitta.

Bitters, Cravings, and Fat Metabolism

Bitters are the missing taste in the modern diet but they are the most common taste in nature. Our ancestors subsisted on diets high in bitters for many, many years. Naturally, in a bitter environment, sweet taste was rare and highly desirable. During these times our taste buds have not yet evolved for modern convenience and availability of sweet taste. Sweets were a rare treat then. Since sweets were desired, it was made available in abundance in modern times and we have started consuming sweets in all kinds of varieties, least realizing the damage it is causing in our system.

Bitters are drying to the body, increases metabolism, and scrapes fat. Bitter purifies the body and dries up all secretions. Bitter resets the taste buds and destroys food cravings. It increases ether element. Therefore, Bitter is recommended in all diets in the Naturopathy aspect.

Qualities of Bitter

Bitters create a descending action that alleviates dizziness and fainting from heat conditions including fevers. Bitters are used to treat fever because they also clear the blood plasma of all impurities (toxins) and sweet taste (mucus kapha) that governs the protective mucus lining of the digestive system. Bitters are light, cooling, clearing and drying. They alleviate pitta and kapha and cleanse the body of toxicity. Bitter taste clears wounds and purifies the skin and muscle tissue.

Word of caution: Excess bitter aggravates Vata causing tissue wasting and hardening, loss of strength and libido, and dryness of the mouth.

Examples of Bitters

Mostly all leafy greens, coffee, orange peel and bitter gourds are bitter. Chocolates are considered bitter although it undergoes significant processing for the bitter taste to be removed. Neem is pure bitter taste and is included as key ingredient in Mahasudarshan and Gymnema Sylvestre. These bitter foods are used for diabetes, to stop food cravings and weight loss. For more info, please logon to www.tammmf.org.

Digestion in the Naturopathy Aspect

In the Naturopathy aspect, digestion does not only, simply mean digestion of food we eat. It also means digesting all the changes that takes place during the preparation of food, while food is being served, while we eat and throughout the assimilation process. Everything that happens to us must be processed. This process is also called digestion. Digestion is, for example, 'digesting' a cold temperature back to 98.6 degrees and, digesting information coming through all the five senses, digesting the joy of eating our favorite food and digesting the pleasure derived from eating. Naturopathy way of digestion is perfect, whole, complete, scientific and total.

Digestion, Imbalance & Healing

Our body naturally maintains balance by protecting itself from changes, be it mild or drastic. Medically, balance is called homeostasis. For example, the body keeps our temperature constant at 98.6 degrees (37°C). In contrast, the environment is always changing. It is this change that usually knocks the body off balance. Disease permeates during this weak situation when we are unable to process change.

Our digestive system's ability to assimilate change is our ability to heal. Proper Digestion is overall healing because digestion sustains balance. Our ability to digest is called "Agni" (digestive fire). Literally, Agni means fire. Anything that remains undigested or stuck in the body is called toxins. Accumulation of toxins affects the balance in our body and this, eventually leads to illnesses.

Truth about Digestion

- Proper Digestion heals.
- Digestion takes work, rest and relaxation.
- It is the Digestive fire that has the ability to digest & heal.
- Toxin is anything we cannot digest that remains stuck in the body for days, months and even years.
- Digestion uses the values in food for the body's balance.
- Gas is a sign of weak digestion.
- We are what we eat and don't poop.
- Digestion starts in the mouth while chewing our food.
- Being conscious about what we eat aids digestion tremendously.

The Magic of Digestion

What is the magic of digestion? The magic of digestion starts the moment we set eyes on the food. Saliva accumulates even before we start eating. The magic continues when we put food into our mouth to be chewed (Mastication). Chewing not only breaks down and crushes very large masses of food molecules and mashes food into smaller particles and allows saliva and enzymes to enter inside the larger food composites, but also triggers off a signaling message to the brain and body to activate the complete digestive process. As mentioned earlier, whatever food that we eat, it becomes a part of our body. And whether the food is hot or cold, acidic or basically alkaline, sugary or bitter, sour or tasteless, the body still has to transform the qualities of the food into the qualities of a human being. When the food that we eat has been properly transformed, the organs and the trillions of cells are nourished, rejuvenated and protected. The most profound way we interact with the environment is by eating from it. Food choices play a central role in our life and are vital in maintaining health and living life to the fullest. It is only by eating the right food that our 4 levels of defense system are kept in constant preparation for attacks by any diseases or foreign matter. Optimum state of our defense system can be attained by only Food.

PHYSICAL DEFENSES
BIOCHEMICAL DEFENSES
IMMUNE SYSTEM
EMERGENCY CONTROLS

Sequential eating

The basic purpose of digestion is retaining energy. This conserved energy is the fuel for our body. Unnecessary digestion consumes energy. Energy must be conserved at any cost as it is the most important factor needed for recovery of health and most of all, it is vital for sustaining life itself. Only sequential eating will optimize the consistent conservation of energy. Energy is needed for almost all functions of our body including burning of calories and guarding from obesity.

Digestion times are much longer and strenuous during;

    i)   a Conventional Diet
    ii) and for persons with sluggish digestive system
    iii) or a person lacking in energy
    iv) and for meals with many ingredients put together randomly and haphazardly
    v) and, not in the optimum sequential order
    vi) and Overeating
    vii) and Variety of food all eaten at one seating
    viii) and Unhealthy food combination.

Therefore, this must be avoided for proper and optimum digestion.

When the quality of food consumed is better, great things will happen to our body and mind. The amazing natural intelligence present in each and every cell of our body and the wisdom of our system in its operation will immediately reveal its amazing self.

Healing by nature – by nature our body is very selectively specific and always seeks to improve towards better health. The body always tries to produce health and always continuously will, unless our interference is too great and overpowering. Only then do we fail to recover and degenerate further into disease.

Our body is designed with a natural mechanism to heal itself. We need not take extensive measures to heal ourselves. Recovering from minor ailments such as colds, fever, cuts, bruises, swellings, injuries etc are examples of how our body tends towards being healthy always – unless we do something to stop the process or do the reverse.

Identifying Food According to its Qualities

Food is not only nutrition. It also has its natural qualities. Naturopathy classifies food by its qualities. Chilies are small but they have a big effect. Different quality has a different effect on our body. There are twenty qualities of food. The twenty qualities are the twenty basic effects of food. Chilies are hot but cucumbers are cool. Bread is heavy but salads are light. Butter is oily but popcorn is dry. Black pepper is intense but cheese is dull. According to Naturopathy, everything is experienced in a mixture of 20 different qualities or attributes, which also describes everything in our physical and mental world.

Dull	Sharp
Hard	Soft
Heavy	Light
Cold	Hot
Wet	Dry
Dense	Subtle
Rough	Smooth
Slow	Quick
Solid	Liquid
Oily	Brittle

An excess or deficiency in one of these qualities can lead to an imbalance in health. These opposing food features are the measuring points for effective diagnosis and treatment of an illness in Naturopathy. Naturopathy believes that if the treatment is like the ailment it's treating, it increases and strengthens that ailment. Only an opposite quality can combat it effectively.

In addition to extracting essential nutrients, our body must neutralize any qualities in the food. If we eat unconsciously, then food can become a toxicant, which goes on to intensely irritate the qualities that are already out of balance. For example, spicy chilies aggravate a high fever. Instead, choose food based on the qualities that will heal or offset the disease.

Naturopathy also classifies food by taste and quality. Every individual needs to create a unique diet that is suitable for the balance in their own body. Therefore, food is our own individual responsibility and not the responsibility of another who does not and cannot relate to the state of another person's body. Diet is very individual and very unique and has to be put together meticulously. Our current trend is that someone else always does the preparation of food for us. Meal is prepared the same way for every member of the family. This is alright up until we come to understand our own body. This is why everyone has come to believe that certain terminal illness is hereditary. Like, if our mother has cancer, the chances are we too will have it, if our father has diabetes, the chances are that we too will have it and one of our grandparents died of a heart attack then the chances are we too might suffer one. All insurance companies are cautious when we fill out our particulars. Our application is bound to be rejected if there is history of cancer, heart attack or diabetes in the family. If all of us in the family eat the same type of food and live the same lifestyle, then we are all bound to end up with the same ailments. Remember, "One man's food is another man's poison"

Guard Our Digestion

Average digestion of food uses up to 60% of our daily metabolism. Digestion takes a lot of work in our system. Since digestion is such a heavy burden on the body's resources, Naturopathy pays attention to the depth of digestion very carefully. Some foods are more difficult to digest than others. Whenever the body is weakened by disease or suffering from indigestion, Naturopathy recommends foods that are easy to digest.

Signs of Indigestion

Signs of food indigestion include constant loud burping, gas, bloated feeling, acid reflux, constipation, and feeling lethargic after eating. Other signs include body odor, bad breath and a thick coating on the tongue.

Gas is generally caused by fermentation of food. Food ferments when it sits in the gut too long. In the process of breaking down and rotting while being in a stagnant state, our food bacteria produce tiny bubbles that collect together and create gas. The formation of gas generally indicates weak digestion.

Pay Attention to our Poop

If good digestion is related to healing then excretion is the measure of health. Many of us flush the evidence without even looking at it. A healthy poop is in the form, size and texture of a matured, ripe banana. Healthy poop is brown in color. Displeasing, foul smelling poop is unhealthy. Healthy elimination includes 1-2 bowel movements a day.

We are what we eat and don't poop. Naturopathy pays close attention to all excretion channels of the body including feces, urine, sweat and breath.

Examine Our poop.....................
It is soooooooooooooo Important.

Examining our poop is one of the best ways to find out what is really going on in our body.

We should take less than 60 seconds to defecate. Typically healthy bowel movement happens no further than 60 seconds of sitting on the throne. The poop should glide out without straining, grunting or any discomfort. It should have the consistency of toothpaste. If we have time to browse a newspaper while sitting on the potty, we probably have a problem with constipation or poor bowel health.

Healthy poop is approximately about four to six inches long and are shaped like a torpedo.

Smaller sized, narrow, pencil-shaped stool is a sign our colon walls are impacted with toxins or we have polyps or growths on the inside of our colon or rectum. This causes the stool to squeeze itself to get through and narrowing its size in diameter. Tensions and stressful situations can also cause **narrow stool**s. Solid, round or pebble-like poop is a potential indication of poor liver function, dehydration, constipation or lack of exercise.

Gas or odor is a sign of bacterial imbalance in our intestinal flora. The "bad" bacteria releases strong smelling gases while the amassed toxins compresses our colon and create awkward odors. We can eliminate this odor by removing the debris and encrusted toxins from the walls of our intestine with the right diet. The right food can, in fact restore the balance in our intestinal flora.

Research indicates that all shades of brown and even green are considered normal poop colors. For example, chlorophyll, beets, tomato juice, green leafy vegetables and excessive artificial colored food that we eat can very much affect the color of our poop. However, a distinguishable change in poop color can be a warning signal for health related complications,

Brown colored poop is normal and it means we have had a healthy, balanced diet followed by healthy bowel movement and elimination.

Yellow colored poop is a sign that our food is moving rapidly through our digestive tract—as in the case of diarrhea. If stool is greasy or foul-smelling, it may indicate excess fat caused by mal-absorption of nutrients.

Green colored poop indicates that optimum assimilation of our food is not happening throughout our digestive tract. Consequently, bile is not broken down—and this gives our poop that green color. Green colored poop can also mean we're eating too much fruits and vegetables, too much sugar and insufficient amount of grains or salt.

Air or bubbles in poop shows an intestinal bacteria imbalance. Gas producing bacteria has the tendency to rapidly grow and may compete with the healthier flora in our gut. Please understand and remember this: *A normal or healthy bowel movement happens within 60 seconds of sitting on the potty. During the job, there should be no forcing, discomfort, bleeding or offensive odor accompanied with our bowel movements. And wiping and cleaning afterwards should be easy and simple using just one or two pieces of toilet paper and then wash!* If this is not what we experience in the toilet every morning then we need to thoroughly cleanse our colon and intestines!

When our colon is in distress, it will do anything and everything to send out signals for health attention! That means giving us the foul breath and unpleasant Body odor! If we notice strong body odor especially under our arm pits or if someone close to us shy away from us and frequently offer us breath refreshing mints, it's time to listen to our colon. It's screaming for help!

Intestinal parasites can also trigger:

  Painful gas and bloating
  Irritable bowels
  Runny stools or diarrhea

Allergies
Skin breakouts
Insomnia
Poor immune system
Muscle pain and joint soreness
And much more……

Digestion can be a massive factor in our life, but in general if we're counting seconds; it is obvious that an average human pooping session takes so much longer than animals. Where is the evolutionary advantage for this time consuming bodily function? It is seen that animals are all much more efficient at it and can do their elimination job effortlessly in matter of seconds.

It is a long time mystery why human alone take ages to defecate. If we observe, we don't see animals straining or grunting and neither do we see any discomfort while they defecate. It has been a lifelong mystery for us as to why it takes such a long time when in actual fact it should all complete in matter of minutes (the bowel movement and cleaning up). If we were caught in the wild somewhere, we would be so vulnerable to ferocious animal attacks if we were to be squatting down for a long time. We need to cultivate the habit squeezing it out smoothly and getting it over and done with, almost immediately. C'mon, life is waiting and we can't be sitting on the pot. But by any chance we do, then of course, it's again time to check our diet. Of course, it's not exactly going to be a party, but it's crucial to educate ourselves about bowel movements — what's unusual, what's expected, what's healthy and what's not. That's because our bathroom behavior can be an important pointer to our overall health: according to research our poop can tell us stories and give us indications of digestive problems, infections, and even early signs of cancer.

So brush up on this important toilet details, and then pay attention to how often we poop, how long we take on the potty, and what the end result looks like and, yes, what it smells like. Simply put, relate to our poop and understand every detail of it. Join a toilet education program with www.tammmf.org.

LOOK BEFORE WE FLUSH

Each poop has a wondrous uniqueness. Do we know what it means? Here's a tell-all tribute to pooh that demystifies the inner workings of the digestive tract and explains our health by what we see in the bowl. Here are some straightforward illustrated and hysterically funny descriptions of our poop. Lets relate with our poop as our poop is one of the barometers to our health.

How hard is it?
Like toothpaste: 1pt
Hard: 2pts

How often do you evacuate?
Once a day: 1pt
Not everyday: 2pts

Feces MUST float, if it sinks, then the nutrients and minerals from food is not completely assimilated
Floats: 1 pt Sinks : 2 pts

2 pieces of feces a day. Each about 2cm in diameter and 15cm in length.
Over 200g: 1pt
Below 200g: 2pts

How long does it take?
Less than 5mins: 2pts
More than 5mins: 1pt

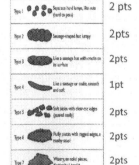

Type 1		Separate hard lumps, like nuts (hard to pass)	2 pts
Type 2		Sausage-shaped but lumpy	2pts
Type 3		Like a sausage but with cracks on its surface	2pts
Type 4		Like a sausage or snake, smooth and soft	1pt
Type 5		Soft blobs with clear-cut edges (passed easily)	2pts
Type 6		Fluffy pieces with ragged edges, a mushy stool	2pts
Type 7		Watery, no solid pieces, Entirely Liquid	2pts

Color of feces
Yellow: 1pt
Brown: 2pts

Does it stink?
Not much: 1pt Bad smell: 2pts

If we scored : 8 pts .....   Good
             9 to 10pts .....We are ok
             11 to 12 pts .....Watch what we eat everyday
             13 to 16 pts....WARNING! If this continues, we are heading towards illness .

The Perfect Food

Advertisers and ambitious entrepreneurs try to sell us miracle foods from far-away places. Everyone has a unique body. For that reason there are no miracle food, that is food for all. We have to pay attention to both our gut (GI tract) and gut feeling before and after eating. The perfect food for us is the food that makes us feel good, light and perfect.

Raw Food versus Cooked Food

Raw food offers nutritional benefits but is more difficult to digest, causing gas and bloating. The nutritional benefits are then outweighed by the toxicity of food fermenting in the gut. Indigestible food is considered poison in Naturopathy. As the saying goes, 'Even the nectar of immortality is a poison if the body can't digest it." Many undercooked foods are hard and chewy, and *hard to chew usually means hard to digest*. The measure of good food is not just its contents, but its interaction with our body.

Cooked food is easier to digest but destroys some vitamins and enzymes during the cooking process. Neither is superior to the other. The real answer to the cooked or raw debate depends on the digestive strength of the individual. Pitta people have the strongest digestive strength and can tolerate more raw foods than others.

Undercooked food often contains parasites. Whether or not the issue is publicized, parasites are common in every country including developed industrialized nations.

Digestive Fire, Toxins and True Hunger

The Digestive fire is digestion of food, experiences or emotions. It creates a feeling of lightness in the body and mind. It creates clarity. Our digestive tract feels clear and our mind experiences clarity of perception. Good Digestive fire is subtle and sattvic, it brings perspective. It literally means a fire. The sanskrit word agni is derived from the same root as the latin word 'ignite'. Agni is drying. And drying here means absorption.

Signs of Good Digestive fire

- Energetic
- Lightness
- Clarity in thoughts
- Brightness in the eyes
- Good appetite
- Regular elimination
- Well formed stools
- Feel rested upon awakening
- Skin has a healthy glow
- Tongue is clear and pink
- Body feels light regardless of the number on the scale
- Feel centered throughout the day
- Digestion is strong without bloating
- Feel energized and enthusiastic
- Mind is clear
- Body has a pleasant smell
- Rarely fall ills

Toxicity is Dull, Tired and Stagnant

Toxicity is loosely translated as toxins in the body. Toxins don't just mean chemicals or corporate waste products. Toxins also mean the residue from improper digestion of food, experiences, and emotions. Toxicity is heavy, oily, gross, cloudy, and sticky. When toxin sticks in the joint spaces, it causes arthritis. Toxicity is tamasic. Our mind becomes clouded by emotions.

Signs of Toxicity

- Bad Breath
- Dull appetite
- Delicate digestion
- Sluggish or irritable elimination
- Generalized pain
- Fatigue
- Depression
- Susceptibility to infection
- Lack of strength, feeling of heaviness, aches and pains.
- Strong and reactive emotions
- Nausea, indigestion, gas or constipation
- Feces with offensive odor or undigested food particles
- Body odor
- Coating on the tongue
- Altered taste buds
- Mucus or post nasal drip
- Gray skin, acne, poor complexion
- Gray, yellow or red eyes
- Urine should be clear and beer colored. Turbid (cloudy) urine is indicated.

Some Common Causes of Toxicity

- Excess fats, proteins, sweets, sour, and salty foods
- Eating too much or too soon after a meal
- Gas, constipation and stagnation of feces in the digestive tract
- Stagnation of urine, sweat or menstruation
- Poor circulation & lymphatic stagnation
- Shock, grief, stress and strong emotions
- Lack of sleep

True Hunger

We are back to true hunger. Learn the difference between an empty stomach and true hunger. Naturopathy says never eat until we get signs of true hunger. We should never eat when emotional or indulge in food as a relief for that matter. The signs or true hunger are:

- Growling stomach.
- Signs of good Digestives fires are especially lightness and clarity.
- Good appetite.

Try to eat before true hunger turns into high pitta, irritability, or low energy and body temperature.

Building Digestive Fire and Burning Toxins

The following activities help to build Digestive Fire and burn Toxins.

- Drink small sips of warm water
- Herbal teas with spices such as ginger, black pepper, fennel, cumin, cinnamon, and cardamom.
- A wedge of lime with a slice of fresh ginger and a pinch of salt before meals.
- Rice & vegetable soups with spices
- Skip a meal or fast for the day until the appearance of true hunger.
- Restorative stretching (strenuous yoga drives Toxins deeper into the tissues) Very light workout is recommended.
- Daily use of Tripala (more info, logon to www.tammmf.org.)

If there is not too much toxins, the following activities will help build strong Digestive Fire

- Light exercise and yoga
- Traditional Massage

Rebuilding Digestive Fire

Soups are the fallback food. Whether under stress, ill, recovering from illness or cleansing, soups give digestive organs a much needed rest. The recommended diet after a Naturopathy treatment is a progression of soups from light to heavy that builds Digestive fires and gradually restore vigor as well. These soups can be served as well to help sick patients rebuild Digestive fires and vigor. This is called Therapeutic diet which literally means a "graded administration of diet". The diet is structured in stages from liquid to gradually increasing solid food called manda, peya, vilepi, odana, yusha, and kichari.

Manda: Rice / Barley Water

Manda means liquid. When sick, most people lose their appetite because that's how our body is designed. Our system needs the rest to recover. Manda is the first meal to be taken when the appetite returns (for about four hours). It is basically water in which basmati or barley is boiled. Use 30 parts of water to 1 part of Basmati rice. It should be served lukewarm with a tsp of ghee and a pinch of black salt.

Peya: Rice / Barley Soup

Peya means soup. Two to three hours later the patient should feel hungry again. Peya is a thin, light porridge. Peya is made with twenty parts water, one part basmati rice or barley and cooked until very soft.

Vilepi: Thick Rice Soup

Vilepi means thick soup. It should be served for the third and fourth meals. Cook with ten parts water to one part basmati rice. Add black salt, a pinch of raw sugar, and sautéed spices in ghee such as ginger, turmeric, cumin, coriander, and fennel.

Odana: Cooked Rice

Odana means cooked rice. It is rice as we know it normally. It should be served at the fifth meal. Odana is cooked 2:1 water to grain. However, only 2tbs is to be served.

Yusha: Mung Lentil Soup

Mung dhal is the easiest to digest compared to all other dhals. Yusha is rice with yellow mung dal added served as a soupy mixture for the 6th meal. Akrita yusha is without spices, fat and salt. Krita yusha is with spices, fat and salt. Use four parts water to ¼ part basmati and 1 part split mung lentils. Recommended spices are black pepper, dry ginger, ghee, and salt.

Kichari: Rice and Daal Mixture

A kitchari is any dish of rice and beans. Rice and beans together provide all twenty amino acids. Fats, carbohydrates and proteins are the building blocks of Vigor. Cooked with ghee, kitchari is vigor building. Kitchari may be eaten for many meals and is very cleansing. It helps with recuperation and rejuvenation. For more info, please logon to www.tammmf.org.

Mamsa Rasa: Meat Juice

Meat based soups provide more vigor but can also create more toxicity. Naturopathy recommends wild animals from a warm, watery climate such as a fish. There are three kinds of meat soups: liquid, medium, and heavy. Four to one mixture of water to meat is liquid. Two and half to one is medium. And two to one is heavy. Akrita rasa is without spices and krita rasa is with spices.

Keep Food Combinations Simple

Although our digestion can get used to some forbidden foods and combinations, anything that aggravates body's toxic levels without expelling them is considered a bad food combination. Generally Vata has the most difficulty with poor food combinations because they do not have enough fluids to adequately break them down. Proper food combination is especially important for anyone with a weakness for food, those recovering from an illness, or those wishing to cleanse or rejuvenate their bodies. One pot meals, preferably soups with a few simple ingredients, are generally the easiest to digest.

Reduce the Enzymes we Need to Digest

Every ingredient demands separate enzymes and attention from the gut. With simpler food combinations our body can focus on each ingredient without too much multi-tasking. Here are some general guidelines:

- Eat only up to three main components in a meal.
- Avoid mixing animal with vegetable proteins.
- Eat proteins with leafy greens only.
- Avoid eating fruits within two hours of a meal. They form a sour wine in the stomach.
- Avoid eating dairy, including cheese, within two hours of a meal. Milk curdles in the stomach if mixed with other foods.
- Rice to be eaten a little later and last.

Do we have Traffic Jam in our Gut?

Eat foods that are easy to digest first, hard to digest last. For example, eat rice before lentils, steamed veggies before nuts. The gut holds onto foods until all the nutrition has been extracted. Every organism loves foods that are easy to digest including the bacteria in our gut. When stuck behind a traffic jam, food that is easy to digest ferments.

Eat Foods with Equal Energetic levels

Is our gut hot and cold at the same time? Although commonly paired in salad cool cucumbers and hot tomatoes don't mix!

Cook the combination

When foods are cooked together their energetic combinations blend together. Soups are easier to digest than salads. Avoid combining raw foods with cooked foods and fresh food with leftovers.

Common Bad Food Combinations to Avoid

Sandwich - The modern sandwich is a newfangled invention by John Montague, the fourth Earl of Sandwich. Obviously the modern sandwich is named after Lord Sandwich. John invented the sandwich while gambling away the long hours of the night. All he needed to survive was bread, meat, cheese and alcohol. Obviously he did not have a very healthy intention behind this invention. Sandwiches are a poor combination because they are generally drying and consumed cold. It contains wheat mixed with meat, raw food with cooked food, and fermented food with fresh.

Cheeseburger - Made with wheat, meat and dairy. Each of these ingredients is difficult to digest separately. Together they confound the stomach causing confusion.

Yogurt with fruit – It's fine to eat them separately as these two combinations are opposites and do not mix well at all. Fruit is sweet and yogurt is sour and yogurt cannot be compared with milk or cheese. Yogurt produces a lot of mucous and when combined with the sugar in fruit, a gooey, sticky substance formulates. The problem with gooey food is that it clogs up the microscopic channels along our gut, blocking enzymes from being released and stopping the proper absorption of nutrients. One point to remember here is that the enzyme to digest milk is released only in the small intestine and not in the stomach. Now that we've mixed up our meal into a big gluey glob of sweet mucous, we are preventing the lactose enzyme from being released. Furthermore, all undigested food ends up being consumed by the bacteria in our gut. This results in gas and toxic waste being excreted by the bacteria in our GI gut.

Contrary to popular believe, Fruit yogurt is NOT a "Healthy Breakfast". We find numerous varieties of premixed yogurt and fruits with loads of added sugar on our supermarket shelves for our "pick up and go" convenience. We actually end up confusing our digestive system with this bad combination.

Although our body is smart, it misinterprets combination of this nature. Here, our body figures out that the milk is not doing any good but what it does not know that it is because of its combination with fruit. Therefore, in order to protect us, our body treats milk as an antibiotic and attacks it the moment it gets into our gastrointestinal tract. Along with this, fruit too is attacked.

Now, let's be clear here, fruit is good for us, yogurt is good for us, and milk too is good for us. But it's NOT good at all when we chop up the fruit and stir it into our yogurt or puree into a smoothie. For those of us who are obsessed with this combination, it's okay to have a bit of it once in a while. But believe it or not, once we refrain and get away from these nasty food combinations, we will develop a natural dislike for them. This combination is allergenic and allergenic foods are addictive, as strange as it may sound. Toxin is produced by the undigested food combination which cannot pass through our impaired colon, thus purging it out through our skin. When this happens, our skin becomes dull looking, dry and develops rashes… (Name it). And here it goes again, "We are what we eat".

Many a times, people who could never give up on certain foods or couldn't live without certain food combinations are doing very well after refraining from it for about 21 days. When our body starts enjoying the right combination, it will automatically reject the wrong combination. This is how we are naturally designed.

We can however, have some fruit early in the morning and have a nice lassi as a mid morning drink. Lassi is a traditional Indian drink where we combine plain curd, with water and spices (like cardamom, or for a more savory taste, cumin) or stevia for sweet taste. We can also do the reverse; have the plain yogurt in the morning and fruit later.

When we avoid the combinations, the food will digest faster. Our body can digest one first, and then digest the other later. We'll reap far more nutrients and energy from them, without the allergenic affects.

Chapattis and Roti Chanai – made with non nutritious flour, vegetable oil and eaten with lentils, meat and chilli paste. Force has to be used even to break up these food with a fork and spoon. Imagine it going down our gut and how our digestive system's struggle to break it down.

Burritos or Wraps - Often contains vegetable with animal proteins (beans and meat). Fillings are mixes of meats with dairy (sour cream and cheese). These wraps contain too many ingredients in general. It has mixtures of raw tomatoes with cooked ones.

Pizza - Mixes wheat with cheese and tomatoes and a whole lot of other stuff in name of a balanced meal.

Apples with peanut butter – Beans and Nuts take a long time to digest. While the body churns away at the bean and nut, the bacteria churns away at the apple which is assimilated much quicker than the beans and nuts.

Salad with tomatoes, cucumbers & raw mushrooms - Contains raw foods of different energetic combinations mixed together.

Time of Meal

The first meal of the day is the spiritual meal of the day. The second meal is the joyful meal. The third meal is the gentle, restorative meal. Our organs are tired after a long day's work and cannot be abused with heavy meals.

Generally, eat first meal at 8am, second meal at noon, and third meal at 5pm. Eat the biggest meal of the day at noon when digestive fire is strongest. Vata may eat smaller meals more often. Kapha can eat fewer meals and skip breakfast altogether. Kapha should never eat heavy foods after sunset. As a matter of fact, we must eat early enough to ensure food will completely digest before sleep. Overnight, undigested food becomes stagnant-blood provoking kapha and mucous. Pitta can eat according to their activity level. Pittas have a natural alarm clock that buzzes when need to eat as they have the strongest digestives fires.

The First Meal

To provide stable nutrition throughout the day, Vata should make sure to include protein in their first meal. An ideal first meal for vata is oatmeal cooked with a 1/4cup of almond meal. Kapha can skip first meal altogether if not hungry. An ideal kapha first meal is a grapefruit with honey. Pitta may eat when hungry.

The Second Meal

Eat the biggest meal of the day during noon. Noon is the warmest time of the day when digestion is strongest. Food eaten during noon has a chance to get digested before bedtime. If we must cheat on our diet program, cheat during the second meal.

The Third Meal

As the body gets tired late in the day so do the digestive organs. Baby the digestion after sunset. The third and last meal should be light and simple.

Guide to Our Organ Timings in Naturopathy

TIME	ORGAN	BODY OPERATIONS
Early Morning 3AM – 5AM	LUNGS	It is good to wake up at this hour. Start off with a 500 ml of mineral or filtered water, not boiled water. The beneficial ozone content in the atmosphere will be more at this time. This will give us a new lease of energy. This is the most appropriate time for breathing exercises, yogasanas and meditation. Asthmatics will have difficulty sleeping at this hour; as such it is recommended that they be up to have a hot nutritious cup of Green Tea or Rooibos Tea.
Morning 5AM – 7AM	COLON (LARGE INTESTINE)	One, who wakes up regularly at this hour, will not suffer from constipation. Drink another 500 ml of mineral water. This is the best time for Bowel Movement. After which a cold shower should also be taken. This regime helps overcome any nervous debility.

Morning **7AM – 9AM**	**STOMACH**	Breakfast, consisting 1 slice of fruit, 1 tbsp of honey, 1 tbsp of apple cider vinegar, ½ tsp cinnamon powder, ½ tsp of black pepper powder, ½ tsp of dry ginger powder, ½ tsp turmeric powder and ½ tsp of garlic powder. Optional: 2 eggs (1 hour later)
Mid **Morning** **9AM–11 AM**	**SPLEEN**	One shall not eat or drink anything during this time, not even a drop of water. If food is consumed at this time, it will increase the body temperature resulting in our body becoming lethargic. The digestive system becomes sluggish and one suffers indigestion. Diabetic patients particularly, may suffer from palpitations and drowsiness.
Noon **11AM–1PM**	**HEART**	Only water should be taken at this time. One shall not do any hard work, nap or sleep at this time, as carbon dioxide may get mixed with oxygen and increases the chances of getting a heart attack, paralytic or severe body ache is high. General practitioners will be on double alert in hospitals during this time because research shows that heart and diabetic patients may suffer a heart attack mostly at this time compared to other times of the day.
Mid Day **1PM–3 PM**	**SMALL INTESTINE**	Great time for lunch – should comprise white meat. It is good to take a 5 minutes rest after lunch just by closing your eyes. Sleep shall be avoided. If we must have an Asian meal, then the proportions should be 6 tbsp vegetable, 2 tbsp meat and 2 tbsp cooked Rice.

Afternoon 3PM–5 PM	**URINARY BLADDER**	This is a good time for a nice cup of Green Tea or Rooibos Tea. Best time for consumption of antioxidants.
Evening 5PM–7 PM	**KIDNEY**	Dinner time – should consist mainly vegetable, preferably green. This is also the time to relax and rest completely. Rest will greatly benefit the renal and urinary tract.
Night 7PM–9 PM	**HEART WALL**	No major meals after this time, otherwise palpitation or chest and stomach discomfort may be experienced.
Late Night 9PM–11PM	**TEMPERATURE (WARMER)**	This is the time that the organs recharge after having worked since morning. Thus one should be sleeping. Must avoid reading, watching TV or working with office files.
Mid Night 11PM–1PM	**GALL BLADDER**	One must be in a state of deep sleep otherwise one will not have the energy for work the next day.
Very Early Morning 1AM– 3 AM	**LIVER**	While liver is cleansing, it is best to be in a state of deep sleep. Otherwise, eye sight may be affected, bad breath and body ache may be experienced

Snacking

Snacking is contraindicated in Naturopathy, especially for kapha. Vata people may need a small snack between meals to prevent hypoglycemia (low blood sugar). If we must snack, snack strategically. Eat light foods that are easy to digest. Wheat crackers, cheese, granola and nuts are generally too heavy for snacking.

Vata Snacks

Avoid drying foods like popcorn, crackers, chips, granola, dried fruits, and nuts. Avoid heavy foods like bread. Ideal vata snacks are liquid and easy to digest.

- Glass of orange juice
- Banana, cooked apple, cantaloupe
- Small bowl of rice puffs
- Pureed carrot soup
- Almond or rice milk

Pitta Snacks

Pitta people have strong digestive fire (digestive strength) and therefore have fewer restrictions on snacking. Ideal pitta snacks are cooling, sweet, and heavy.

- Almond milk
- Cucumber milk
- Pomegranates, grapes, raw apple

Kapha Snacks

Kapha can snack on dry, light, unsalted foods.

- Pear, raw apple, watermelon
- Celery sticks
- Popcorn
- Peeled pumpkin seeds relieves but slows down eating

Desserts

Healthy Options for Homemade Desserts

Although unhealthy, people crave something sweet during the sour and salty phases of digestion, for at least one to two hours after a meal. The eyes sting slightly and the mind becomes irritable during this phase. This is when we opt for a sweet dessert. However, it must be understood that Dessert mixes with the partially digested dinner, disturbing digestion and the process of assimilation.

Therefore opt for following healthy options:

- Use raw sugar, agave, maple syrup, date sugar, bananas, or raisins instead of refined sugar. Fruit and natural sugars are much less aggravating to Vata, Pitta and Kapha.
- Here's a way to halve the sugar quantity in most dessert recipes. Sprinkle a bit of sugar on the top or bottom of cookies. When taste buds touch the sugar, the whole cookie tastes sweet.
- Use spelt flour instead of refined flour. Refined flour is sticky and clogs the GI tract. Refined flour is much harder to digest and kapha provoking.
- Use ghee instead of oil. Ghee is light. Ghee is better than all oils. It is the easiest fat to digest. Butter to be the second choice followed by coconut oil and olive oil.

- Use sweet spices to make the cookie more digestible. Sweet spices are spices that work particularly well for dessert. They balance the heavy, dull, cold, gooey qualities of dessert foods. Some examples of sweet spices include cinnamon, cardamom, ginger, nutmeg, fennel and cloves.
- Serve desserts warm instead of cold. Warm foods are easier to digest.
- When indulging in dessert, eat in small quantities very slowly. Take the time to completely relish and enjoy it.

Eat Slowly with Contemplation on the Food

Naturopathy recommends concentration on the taste of food while eating. Eating unconsciously causes poor food choices and portions. Avoid other activities while eating such as walking, driving, watching TV, or talking. In general, Naturopathy avoids multi-tasking. Any activity definitely redirects blood from digestion into other organs.

Eating food slowly also gives the following benefits:

- Encourages thorough chewing
- Give taste buds and the nose a chance to decipher what's been eaten.
- Helps regulate portion size by giving cravings a chance to catch up.

Drink Food and Chew Water

The meaning of drink food and chew water is to be understood as, we have to chew our food till its watery and soft and water is to be drank slowly, mixed with saliva before swallowing. All foods that are difficult to digest must be chewed with care. Insufficient chewing of food forces stomachs to break down larger chunks by acids. While this is an easier task for our tooth, it however takes time and effort for the acids in our stomach. Remember, the teeth are in the mouth not in the digestive tract. Therefore complete chewing has to done in the mouth before swallowing. In the hot, balmy environment of the gut, digestion is delayed and, delays in digestion lead to fermentation. Hard to chew means hard to digest.

Chew food, even drinks, until it is completely mixed with saliva. Saliva contains enzymes that help digest food. Saliva also fights bacteria. Proper chewing alerts the tonsils and the immune system to threats by bacteria.

Drink Water Before a Meal, Not During

Water before a meal is nectar. It replenishes fluids and encourages juicy digestive organs. Small sips of honey are recommended during a meal. It makes food easily digestible. On the other hand, water immediately after a meal is "poison" as it dilutes stomach acids exerting digestion.

Like all foods, water must be digested until it resembles the blood in salinity, sweetness, and ph level. Water takes effort to digest but doesn't provide nutrition. Naturopathy recommends broths instead of water during meals. Some examples are soup stocks, almond smoothies, and fruit juices. Water is to be taken throughout the day and NOT during meals. If the food we eat is chewed thoroughly, then we do not need water to wash it down.

A Handful is Healthy Portion

The proper portion of food is the volume of our two hands making a cup together. After eating, the stomach should be 1/3 food, 1/3 liquid, and 1/3 empty. Empty space in the stomach gives the stomach room to digest. Overstuffing the stomach causes partially digested food to enter into the duodenum too quickly and leads to ulcers.

Rest on the Left Side After Eating

After eating, blood rushes to the stomach to supply stomach glands with fluids. The food is mixed with acids and slowly turns into a thick broth. About fifteen minutes after eating, the food is fully hydrated and blood flow to the stomach relaxes somewhat. To ensure a proper supply of blood, rest at least fifteen minutes after eating. Lie on the left side to help food stay in the upper portion of the stomach. Avoid sleeping, studying, exercise and sex for two hours after eating.

Seasons Eating

Late Winter / Spring - Mid-January - Mid May

The spring is a watery season of warming temperatures. Snow melts making the rivers full and muddy. Cold atmosphere turns warm and encourage tender sprouts and sweet sap to run in the vasculature of maple trees. Our internal landscape reflects Mother Nature. Spring is a time of cleansing and renewal. Kapha fat melts away from tissues, along with toxins, and into the blood, making the blood sweet. Blood plasma and toxins are our metaphorical maple syrup and Muddy River, releasing a flood of mucus in allergy season.

Summer - Mid-May to September

Dry Summer Climates - The summer sun dehydrates the bodily tissues, reduces appetite and aggravates pitta. Eat a pitta pacifying diet with sweet, oily, cold and liquid foods making sure they are light for digestion. Avoid pungent and sour tastes.

Humid Summer Climates - Hot, humid weather is irritable weather and causes rashes, irritability, and lethargy. Eat a pitta and kapha pacifying diet favoring cold and astringent. Avoid alcohol, other ferments and sour taste. Favor bitters instead. Tikta Ghrta is a popular herb formula to reduce pitta and kapha in humid summer months. For more info, please logon to www. tammmf.org.

Autumn/Early Winter: September - January

Cooling temperatures pull blood inward to the core as the body scrambles to protect itself from heat loss. The extremities lose access to blood and warmth, drying out the skin on the arms, legs and eventually the colon. The core of the body enriches with blood, conversely, improves appetite just in time to nourish and insulate the skin with a fresh layer of fat.

Rice

Every day we hear people say, *"rice is no good"*, *"rice is the root cause for all diseases"*, *"we should stop eating rice"*, *"we can never be healthy with rice"*, *"rice is processed grain"*, *"eating rice is equivalent to eating sugar"*, *"we should cut down on rice"* and *"rice is the culprit in our diet"*. The same person, who tells us that rice is no good, is not able to name a better substitute for rice. When pressed for an answer, they go with Chapatis, roti pratas, bread, noodles, soups etc.

Rice is Asian's food and Asians themselves are condemning rice. For centuries we have been maintaining good health with rice. As a matter of fact, our parents, grandparents and great grandparents were fairly lean with rice compared to us to have reduced rice substantially from our diet and enjoy obesity rather than health. Obesity is common these days although we are trying to do away with rice. This is because we have westernized our food. We have moved from what we are supposed to eat to what we are proposed to eat. These factors are deranging our metabolisms, turning the fairly friendly rice into an enemy.

Carbohydrates by themselves are friendly in our metabolic vacuum. If we have everything inside us in order and going right, then rice will not pose a big problem. Of course, a 40 something mother of 4 who's a working wife and overweight and has an issue with glucose may need to drastically cut down on rice. This too is because, we have set it in our mind that diabetes will not be cured in a lifetime and can be only kept "under control". Rice in our meal depends on where we fall on the metabolic derangement order.

We have to face facts that we live in an era where "out of order" health has become normal; Diabetes is standard, Obesity is normal, Arthritis is common, Everybody falls ill, Hospital appointments are a way of life, Poor eye sight at 40 is normal, Doctors know best and Rice is bad.

Rice Facts

Rice is the source for 25% of global human energy. Half the world population depends on Rice as their staple diet. On an average, even an American eats about 10kgs of rice per year. Asians eat as much as 150kgs per year, while Arabs eat about 230kgs and the French about 5kgs per year. Everybody eats rice.

Rice is the most available food for millions of people around the globe. If not for rice, half the world will be starved to death. So for God sake, **GIVE RICE THE DUE RESPECT.**

The Food Proportion Proper

The right Eating Order – *1st the apple, 2nd the vegetable, 3rd the meat and 4th the 2 tbsp of rice.*

Some nutritionists very forcefully say that the human body was never meant to consume rice. The arguments of these modern day nutritionist are that Caveman never ate rice. Rice was not part of ancient man's food. We have to accept that, our genes may not have changed too much since ancient times. However, our food choices and lifestyle have changed tremendously. Our food choices changed not because we listened to our body's needs (inward) but because we listened to anything and everything anyone says about good food (outward). Some experts say that the pre-historic man would hardly recognize our current food or our current way of life, true but then again why should he? He is not in our modern world and we are not in the ancient time. We have evolved. There is an evolution taking place every moment and we have to flow with the currents and not against it. Our lifestyle has changed. We are not swinging from tree to tree. We don't even look like caveman anymore. Our features, structure and build is not the same as caveman anymore. We have evolved into beautiful creations if compared with caveman.

If we were to cut out rice completely from our diet and call it the culprit that causes diseases and shift to "better" food (whatever that may be that our experts say), Then who will eat rice? If the rich and well-to-do people remove rice from their meal and substitute it with other more healthy and expensive option, what do the poor eat? Rice is the food the poor can afford. Looking at the statistic below, we understand that the ratio of people from poverty to wealthy level is 93 to 1. Where will the balance be? It would be totally selfish to say that rice is bad and one should STOP eating it. We all should cut down on rice…. drastically but never stop simply because we co-exist with people who cannot afford a healthy lifestyle that does not include rice. Here is something to jolt our mind; if we have our a wedding dinner, what do we serve? Do we serve a platter of nutritious food without rice? If someone hungry comes up to us and asks for food, what do we buy them? Rice definitely! We do not take them back home and cook them nutritious food without rice do we? So where is the balance? Why the double standards? It is not practical at all. Does it make sense at all? We need the natural balance in everything we do, both internally and externally.

World Poverty Statistics

Statistic Verification	
Source: Global Issues, The Human Development Report	
Research Date: 7.23.2012	

World Poverty Statistics	
Total Percentage of World Population that lives on less than $2.50 a day	50%
Total number of people that live on less than $2.50 a day	3 Billion
Total Percentage of People that live on less than $10 a day	80%
Total percent of World Populations that live where income differentials are widening	80%
Total Percentage of World Income the richest 20% account for	75%
Total Number of children that die each day due to Poverty	22,000
Total Number of People in Developing Countries with Inadequate Access to Water	1.1 billion
Total Number of School Days lost to Water Related Illness	443 million schooldays
Child World Poverty Statistics	
Number of children in the world	2.2 billion
Number of Children that live in Poverty	1 billion
Total Number of Children that live without adequate shelter	640 million (1 in 3)
Total Number of Children without access to safe water	400 million (1 in 5)
Total Number of Children with no access to Health Services	270 million (1 in 7)
Total Number of Children who die annually from lack of access to safe drinking water and adequate sanitation	1.4 million

Poverty to Wealthy Ratio Statistics	
Year	Ratio of People at Poverty to Wealthy Level
1820	3 to 1
1913	11 to 1
1950	35 to 1
1973	44 to 1
1992	72 to 1
2001	82 to 1
2012	93 to 1

The arguments of our modern day nutritionist are that Caveman never ate rice. Caveman's food was never cooked as fire was not yet found. Thus, he ate only those foods that can be eaten without treatment with or by fire. He would never understand cooking. He ate fruits, vegetables, fish, eggs, nuts and meat. Yes, even raw meat! We too can eat raw meat if we were starving in the forest. We have the necessary enzymes to digest raw meat. Yes, we do have the enzymes to digest meat but we have moved forward to cooking and there is no need for us to eat raw meat. Most experts say that we were never meant to eat Rice, wheat and other grains because it cannot be eaten raw. Then again, why should we eat it raw? And this does not mean we were never meant to eat rice. It is just that just we need to cut rice down to very small portions. Today rice has become our staple food. We have to eat rice if we live amongst other human being. It is just that instead of only eating loads of rice, we opt for a balanced blend, and not make rice the bulk of our daily diet.

One thing we all should remember when arguments arise about Caveman not eating rice is their Life span. Caveman's life span was 35 to 40 years only. Our Life span to-date is an average of 77 years. This is more than double the age of Caveman. This is a rice era and longevity is established.

In some Asian countries, rice form 85% to 90% of the meal. It is good to keep rice we eat to a bare minimum. 2 table spoonful of (cooked rice) the most at each meal. When we reduce rice drastically, our eating pattern too will change drastically for the better. Remember, rice is good for the tongue more than the body. Rice and other grains like wheat and corn are actually worse than sugar. Therefore keep it to a bare minimum.

The reasons why rice must be reduced are:

- Rice is carbohydrate. Carbohydrate is sugar. Rice becomes sugar and spikes circulating blood sugar within half an hour - almost as quickly as it would if we took a sugar candy. So it's ridiculous to cut down sugar in our teh tarik and coffee while eating lots of rice. A bowl of rice is equivalent to 10 teaspoons of sugar.

- Rice is very low in anti-oxidants. Complete anti-oxidant components are necessary for the effective and safe utilization of sugar. Fruits, however, come with a sugar called fructose and they are not empty calories as the fruit is packed with a whole host of other nutrients that help its proper assimilation throughout the digestion process.

- White rice has no fiber; we end up eating lots of 'calorie dense' food before we get filled up. Brown rice has more fiber but still the same amount of sugar. Brown rice is only slightly better than white rice, contrary to popular belief.

- We can never eat anything as much as we can eat rice. Be it sugar, vegetable, meat or fish, we can eat only so much before hurling up. Rice is the only food for which we do not have a mechanism that says enough.

- Since there is no real 'built in' mechanism inside us to prevent us from overeating of rice, we need to be conscious, absolutely conscious when eating rice. Conscious of the fact that each bowl of rice is 10 teaspoons of sugar. Some of us can eat up to 5 bowls of rice that directly translates to 50 teaspoons of sugar. The best part is, we ask for tea with less sugar ("teh tarik kurang manis") at the end of a banana leaf meal or "thali" meal. This clearly shows that we don't know our food qualities at all.

- Eating rice causes us to eat more salt because rice cannot be eaten by itself. It has to be eaten with condiments. Therefore, end each meal with just 2 tablespoons of rice. Lots of food enhancers like MSG, sugar, ketchup, chili sauce and soy sauce that is salty, preserved and sweet is needed with rice as rice by itself is tasteless.

- Eating rice causes us to drink less water. We do not feel thirsty for a long time after eating rice. The more rice we eat, the less water we tend to drink.

- Rice is known to prevent the absorption of several vitamins and minerals. When taken in bulk, it reduces the absorption of vital nutrients like zinc, iron and the B vitamins.

o   We tend to overeat when it comes to rice. At any one meal, our
    stomach should be loaded with approximate 500gm of food (minus
    water). This would allow optimum digestion at a relaxed pace and we
    will not develop a protruded belly. One would not experience the after-
    meal tiredness. (Caution)But then again, the stomach can also expand
    up to 6kgs for food consumption with rice. This is when disruption
    during digestion takes place and we can very easily put on a pot belly.
    There is a need for us to maintain the right body size. Again, body
    size differs for everyone. Uncomfortable body size leads to numerous
    health complications.

When we Transform from Hazardous Unhealthy State to Healthy Comfortable State ....

Migraine < 57%

Pressure inside the skull < 96%

Abnormal amount of Cholesterol < 63%

Abnormal retention of fat in Liver < 90%

Liver Inflammation < 37%

Fibrosis in Liver < 20%

Metabolic Syndrome < 80%

Diabetes < 83%

Hormonal Imbalance in women < 79%

Menstrual Dysfunction < 100%

Quality of Life Improved 95%

Depression < 55%

Disordered breathing during sleep < 74-98%

Asthma 82% resolved

Cardiovascular Disease < 80%

Hypertension < 52-92%

Gastritis < 72-98%

Incontinence < 44-88%

Osteoarthritis <41-76%

Gout < 77%

Sleep Disorder < 89%

Improper functions of veins in the leg < 95%

The Overall Quality of Our Life IMPROVES

Ragi - The Better Option

Ragi is considered the "poor man's food" in Asian countries. Ragi cherry is one of the best semi-solid foods that we can give our kid before we get him used to solid food. However, this is available only in India. It's the best strengthening baby food that we can ever give our weaning baby. Ragi is also a rich source of fiber and helps lower cholesterol level. Ragi is best food for weight control, diabetes and has a cooling effect on our body. Ragi may sound alien to many as it is a forgotten staple food since rice took over. Speak to our great granny and am sure she will tell us the goodness of ragi and also give us many ragi recipe suggestions that includes dosa, vermicili, kanji, malt, ragi balls, ragi bread and a whole other range. With its cost-effectiveness, our great grandmothers will definitely endorse that ragi is definitely a health food that has loads of goodness.

Nutritional Comparison of RICE and RAGI

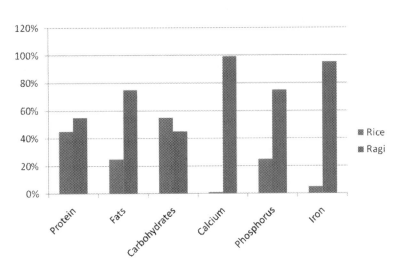

Health Benefits of Ragi

Ragi, more commonly known as finger millet is a cereal grown in India and as mentioned earlier, at one point of time Ragi was India's staple food till rice took over. This crop easily and naturally grows at altitudes higher than usual making it more organic. It is one of the few cereals that need not be polished making it healthier than most of all other cereals. Here are a few more reasons to include this wonder grain in our diet:

Rich in calcium – Start replacing expensive calcium pills with a nourishing ragi kanji or porridge and moreover, including it in the diet of growing children is a great way to reap its benefits. Till to-date, there is not another cereal that comes close to ragi where calcium content is concerned. Calcium is a significant factor in our diet and most of us tend to swear by branded and advertised calcium tablets. Calcium is vital when it comes to bone development and prevention of osteoporosis. Try replacing calcium pills with ragi meals.

Helps in weight loss – Ragi contains an amino acid called Tryptophan which reduces appetite substantially. After eating ragi in any cooked form, we'll have a feeling of fullness for quite some time. The natural fat content in ragi is very much lower than all other cereals. Also, this fat is in its unsaturated form which is also good for us. Thus, substituting it for wheat and rice is an excellent choice if we are trying to lose weight.

High fibre content – is excellent for people with high cholesterol. Ragi contains Threonine that hinders the formation of fat in the liver and provides overall reduction of body cholesterol. There are two amino acids in ragi known as, Lecithin and Methionine. Both help in decreasing the cholesterol levels of our body by getting rid of the excess fat that forms in the liver. As compared to white rice, or the preferred brown rice, ragi contains much higher amounts of dietary fibre. Due to this, ragi aids digestion, prevents over-eating and makes us feel full for a longer span of time.

Methionine	Methionine is an amino acid. Amino acids are the building blocks that our bodies use to make proteins. Methionine is found in meat, fish, and dairy products, and it plays an important role in many cell functions. Methionine is used to prevent liver damage in acetaminophen (Tylenol) poisoning. It is also used for increasing the acidity of urine, treating liver disorders, and improving wound healing. Other uses include treating depression, alcoholism, allergies, asthma, copper poisoning, radiation side effects, schizophrenia, drug withdrawal and Parkinson's disease. ***How does it work?*** In acetaminophen poisoning, methionine prevents the breakdown products of acetaminophen from damaging the liver.
Threonine	Threonine is an amino acid. Amino acids are the building blocks the body uses to make proteins. Threonine is used to treat various nervous system disorders including spinal spasticity, multiple sclerosis, familial spastic paraparesis, and amyotropic lateral sclerosis (ALS, Lou Gehrig's disease). ***How does it work?*** Threonine is changed in the body to a chemical called glycine. Glycine works in the brain to reduce constant and unwanted muscle contractions (spasticity).

Lecithin	Lecithin is a fat that is essential in the cells of the body. It can be found in many foods, including soybeans and egg yolks. Lecithin is taken as a medicine and is also used in the manufacturing of medicines.
	Lecithin is used for treating memory disorders such as dementia and Alzheimer's disease. It is also used for treating gallbladder disease, liver disease, certain types of depression, high cholesterol, anxiety and a skin disease called eczema.
	Some people apply lecithin to the skin as a moisturizer.
	We will often see lecithin as a food additive. It is used to keep certain ingredients from separating out.
	We may also see lecithin as an ingredient in some eye medicines. It is used to help keep the medicine in contact with the eye's cornea. How does it work? Lecithin is converted into acetylcholine, a substance that transmits nerve impulses.

Source: www.webmd.com

Aids diabetics – Diabetics can trust ragi to create a restrained environment in the building-up of glucose level after meals. The added perk that all of us will enjoy is of course the high fiber content and high polyphenol. Diets that regularly include ragi have been known to have tremendously lower glycemic response. The dietary fibre in ragi is higher than all other grains simply because of the inclusion of bran in ragi as the grain is too small to be polished and milled.

Battles anemia – Great remedy for those of us who constantly suffer spasm attacks. Many of us suffer from these cramps especially in the feet and hands and sometimes in other parts of the body. Although these muscle cramps are usually harmless and ceases after a few minutes, the excruciating pain is sometimes unbearable. Depending on when and where we get these attacks is embarrassing too. Just change our diet from rice to ragi and experience the difference immediately. This is because Ragi is an excellent source of natural iron. Patients of anaemia and low haemoglobin levels can begin to include ragi in their diets as a domestic remedy. Vitamin C is known to aid the absorption of iron. Once ragi is allowed to sprout, the vitamin C levels increase and lead to further absorption of iron into the bloodstream.

Ragi is a Natural relaxant – The surplus amount of amino acids and ample amount of antioxidants in ragi help the body to naturally relax. Common discomforts like anxiety, insomnia, headaches and depression can be reduced and eliminated with ragi. The major contributor to the relaxing effects of ragi is the amino acid called Tryptophan.

Reduces the risk of stroke – Ragi cherry is excellent meal for one who has suffered a stroke. Ragi, in its early stages of growth, that is, when it is still green, can help prevent high blood pressure. The cholesterol levels in blood can be regulated too, leading to less plaque formation and blockage of vessels. With ragi as part of our diet, the risk for hypertension and stroke goes down significantly.

Gluten-free – Not many cereals can boast of this property since gluten is a major nutrient in all cereals. If we find a gluten free cereal, we have to pay a hefty price for it. People suffering from celiac disease or followers of the gluten-free diet can incorporate ragi into their daily consumption as it is completely free of gluten.

Excellent baby food – In India, where ragi is widely consumed, babies as old as 1 month old are fed with ragi porridge as introduction to semi solid food. It is believed that ragi actively encourages better digestion. The high calcium and iron content supports and compliments the bone growth and overall development of the infant. Specially-processed ragi powders for infants are available to be used during weaning. For more information, please logon to www.tammmf.org.

Boosts lactation – Breast feeding (Lactating, nursing) mothers are urged to include ragi, especially when it is green as it enhances milk handling and enriches the milk with the essential amino acids, iron and calcium required for the nutrition of the mother as well as the child. The production of milk is also affected positively. Ragi is prescribed to the mothers that wish to increase the quantity of milk produced for their baby.

Nutritional Comparison of RICE and RAGI

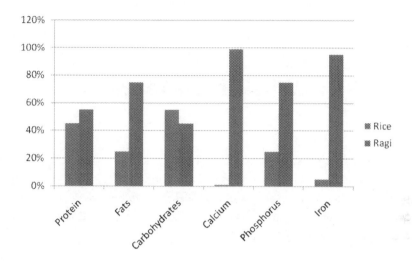

Why Green Tea?

Green tea needs no introduction. We have to consume green tea to discover the health benefits of green tea. Green tea is good for the overall functioning of the body as it is rich in antioxidants. Weight watchers swear by green tea. The Chinese believe that, it's "**Better to be deprived of food for three days, than tea for one**".

This tea has been the subject of many scientific and medical studies to determine its many health benefits. It is least processed, provides the most antioxidant polyphenols, specifically a catechin called epigallocatechin-3-gallate (EGCG), which is responsible for most of the health benefits.

- It is known to inhibit the growth of cancer cells and also helps in extinguishing dangerous cells without harming any healthy cell. This greenish-yellow tea that has a raw, slightly astringent flavor close to the taste of the fresh leaf instantly relaxes our nervous system.
- Green tea improves total cholesterol levels, as well as balances the ratio of good cholesterol to bad cholesterol. Moreover, it inhibits the abnormal formation of blood clots which is the leading cause of heart attacks and stroke. Green tea represses angiotensin II which leads to high blood pressure & reduces the possibilities of heart attacks.
- Green tea help in preventing bad breath and tooth decay. As the bacteria destroying abilities of green tea helps in preventing food poisoning, it can also kill the bacteria that cause dental cavities.
- Green tea lowers the risk for a wide range of diseases, from simple bacterial or viral infections to chronic disease.
- Green tea stabilizes sugar level in a body and is good for diabetics. The polyphenols present in green tea extract reduces the amount of amylase produced by conversion of starch into sugar and hence the levels of sugar in the blood also decrease.

- One of the best advantages of green tea is weight loss. Its natural with only one side effect, that is – we will look and feel better. Yes, this is the ONLY side effect.

- Green tea helps in burning the fat & increasing metabolism naturally due to one of its contents called catechin polyphenols. With this, cholesterol is lowered & fat oxidation is enhanced.

  Moreover weight is gained as excess sugars and fats are stored in the body as fat cells. Green tea catechin helps in preventing obesity by inhibiting the movement of glucose in fat cells.

  Contains EGCG - that is a powerful antioxidant with positive qualities that is important for any health disorder.

- Green tea has an antibacterial and antiviral agent. It helps during influenza and diarrhea. It relieves stress, improves bone structure and delays the onset of osteoporosis.
- Green tea relaxes us and helps in getting relief from depression & headache which is a common problem of a common man in this era.

Green tea is a very useful variety of tea as opposed to other tea that contains tannin which is known to harden protein.

Super Rooibos Tea

ROOIBOS SOD TEA is a caffeine free tea and has the lowest tannin content in comparison with any other tea. It has an instant soothing effect on the central nervous system which completely translates to total relaxation. This tea contains a very strong anti oxidant agent that is not found in other tea that which slows down the aging process and improves the immune system.

ROOIBOS SOD TEA contains 50 times more SOD in comparison with any other tea. It also supplements our daily amount of calcium especially fluoride which is required for the development of strong bones and teeth.

Simple perfect way to brew ROOIBOS SOD TEA;

1. Rinse teapot (preferably ceramic) with boiling water.
2. Place 1 sachet into teapot – 1 teabag can brew up to 1.5 liters of tea.
3. Pour boiling water onto teabag and allow infusion for 2 – 3 minutes.
4. Enjoy the soothing tea, plain, just like that or sugar, creamer can be added.

Recommended consumption: At least 1 sachet a day.

Beneficial Images Of Rooibos Tea

From the Research Substantiates of Dr. Charlene Marais Phd., (Chem.) University of the Free State, South Africa.

Nutrients	Function In The Body
Iron	Essential for transporting of oxygen in the blood
Potassium	Necessary for metabolic function
Copper	Necessary for different metabolic processes
Calcium	Necessary for strong teeth and bones
Manganese	Necessary for metabolic processes and for bone growth and development
Fluoride	Necessary for healthy teeth and bones
Zinc	Necessary for normal growth and development and a healthy skin
Magnesium	Necessary for a healthy nervous system and for other metabolic processes
Sodium	Necessary for fluid and acid-base balance
Rooibos Metabolites	**Physiological And Therapeutical Activities**
Terpinen – 4-ol	Analgesic, Antiallergenic, Antiasthmatic, antibacterial, expectorant, hypotensive, vasodilator
Eugenol	Antibacterial, antiyeast, hypothermic, antioxidant, skeletal muscle relaxant, anticonvulsant, CNS depressant
Ferulic acid	Antibacterial, antifungal, antiyeast, antiarrhythmic, antihepatoxic, antitumour, antiocstrogenic
Quercetin	Antiviral, antineoplastic, antioxidant, antispasmodic
Myrcene - terpincol	Antiasthmatic, vasodilator, hypotensive
Caffeic acid	Antibacterial, antifungal, Antiviral, antihepatoxic,
Protocatechuic acid	Antibacterial, antifungal, Antiviral, myocardial O2 consumption decreaser, antihepatoxic,

(+)-Catechin	Antibacterial, antihepatoxic, Antiabaphylactic, Anticoagulant, Homeostatic, Epaloprotective, Anticholestermic
(+)-Pinitol	Expectorant, Antidiabetic
Vannillic acid	Antihelmintic
p-Hydroxybenzoic acid	Antimutagenic
Uridine	Relieve symptoms of orotic acid-uria
Superoxide Dismutase (Sod) Enzyme	**Anti-aging**
Rutin (vit P)	Reinforces and stabilizes blood vessels.
Ascorbic acid (vit C)	Relieve symptoms of Scurvy

Caffeine & Tannin Content (1 Tea Bag)
Comparison of Control over Strength Of Lipid Peroxides

Drinks	Caffeine (mg)	Tannin (%)	Enzymatic activity of SOD in units (preventing the production of lipid peroxides in the blood cells.
Rooibos Tea	0	1	72,615
Coffee	60 to 150	4.60	12,453
Wheat Tea	60 to 90	7 to 15	607
Woolong Tea	60 to 90	7 to 15	1,992
Green Tea	15 to 43	7 to 15	1,450
Black or Red Tea	19 to 39.3	7.18 to 13	780

Sources & References:

> Department of Food Science, University of Stellenbosch, South African.
> America Chemical Society, Washington.
> Department of Medicine, Microbiology Section, University of Kumamoto, Japan.
> Journal Korean Society Food Nutrition, Korea.
> Encyclopedia of Herbal Medicine (Thomas Bartram)

Rooibos Tea Can Assist us as a Supplement to Our Food

Our human body's anti-acid substances known as SOD (Super -oxide Dismutase) provides substantial resistance to chronic diseases. But as age catches up, this will eventually prove ineffective. Hence a supplement of SOD is essential especially for the following conditions;

1) *Feeling irritated for no reasons*
2) *Mild or acute headaches*
3) *Irregular sleeping patterns*
4) *Insomnia*
5) *Feeling nervous and tensed*
6) *Mild depression*
7) *Hypertension*
8) *Heartburn*
9) *Stomach ulcers*
10) *Constipation*
11) *Stomach cramps*
12) *Colic in infants*
13) *Asthma*
14) *Eczema*
15) *Itching*
16) *Nappy rash*
17) *Acne*
18) *Anti aging*
19) *Removing uric acid(main cause for aches and pains)*
20) *Rheumatism*
21) *Gout*

22) *Neutralizes harmful free radicals,*
23) *Stabilizes body immunity*
24) *Improves normal body functions*
25) *Improves skin complexion*
26) *Helps with kidney stones (yes,* www.tammmf.org*)*
27) *Reduces cholesterol*
28) *Increases resistance against diseases*
29) *Gastritis*
30) *Water retention, swollen feet*
31) *Migraine*
32) *Urinary tract infection or other related problems*
33) *Diabetes*
34) *Regulates blood pressure*
35) *Restore vital body fluids*
36) *Builds health and energy*
37) *Replenishes iron levels*
38) *Good for breast feeding mothers*
39) *Good for pregnant women*
40) has a soothing effect on the central nervous system
41) and most of all, **There Is Absolutely No Side Effect!**

Simple Ways of Detecting Nutritional Deficiencies

Our Hands	If our Hands feel Cold	Magnesium deficiency, hypothyroidism, chronic fatigue with low cardiac output
Our Nails	When we see white spots on our nails	Mineral deficiency, but often low zinc
	When Ridges form	Zinc deficiency
	When our nails become Soft or brittle nails	Magnesium deficiency
	When nails are bitten	General mineral deficiency

Our Skin	Stretched marks	Zinc deficiency
	Skin condition called Follicular Hyperkeratosis	Vitamin A deficiency
	Spontaneous Bleedings	Vitamin C or K or platelet deficiency
	Very Dry scaly skin with hair follicles plugged with coiled distorted hairs and a tiny red halo	Vitamin C deficiency
	When our palms are yellow	Excessive beta carotene intake
	When our skin at the upper back is pimply and rough skin "chicken skin"	Essential fatty acid deficiency
Our Face	Reddish, Greasy, scaly skin on face and sides of nose	Vitamin B2 deficiency
	Tiny Acne like rash around nose and forehead	Vitamin B6 deficiency
Our Eyes	Cataracts formation	Chromium deficiency or excess free radicals
	Eye Bags or dark circle under eyes	Allergies or food intolerances
	Bluish eyes or premature grey hair	Vitamin B12 deficiency, a feature of pernicious anemia
Our Legs	Sore calf muscles and active knee reflexes	Magnesium deficiency
Our Heart	Enlarging of heart, Irregular beat, High Blood pressure,	Magnesium and CoQ10 deficiencies or sensitivity to caffeine

Our Mouth	Pale, scrotal tongue	Iron deficiency
	Sore, painful scrotal tongue	Vitamin B3 deficiency
	Sore, stingy tongue and peeling of lips	Vitamin B2 deficiency
	Swollen tongue with lateral teeth indentations	Food intolerance
	Painful, sore tongue with a smooth appearance	Folic acid deficiency
	Cracked lips	Vitamin B2 deficiency. Thrush.
Our Throat	Swelling in our throat	Iodine deficiency, hypothyroids

Understanding our Body's Natural Biorhythms

A balanced diet, sound regular sleep coupled with sufficient exercise, reducing our daily toxic threshold, cleansing our body regularly with Naturopathy fasting, and maintaining a positive state of mind are required to obtain an optimum health state. The first step in any diet plan is to understand how the body utilizes and processes the nutrients it needs. Understanding the biorhythms that are regulating our body's nutritional needs is crucial. All creatures on this planet, including human beings, are naturally attuned to three daily body cycles. These cycles have precise and established hours set by the laws of nature.

The Elimination Cycle

This Cycle Begins approximately 04:00 hours and ends around 12:00 hours.

During this cycle of the day, our body naturally tries to expel itself of toxic waste materials and unnecessary salts, proteins, and acids. During this cycle period we should consume adequate amounts of fresh seasonal fruit (preferably locally grown) to support the body's natural toxin elimination cycle. Not only does fruit supply the body with living matter to draw out unwanted substances, it also ensures the intestinal tract remains well hydrated and nourished. Fresh raw fruit provides the ideal ingredients for supporting the body's Elimination Cycle.

The Energy Cycle

This Cycle Begins approximately 12:00 hours and ends at about 20:00 hours

During the Energy Cycle, food and nutrients are processed and stored to provide us with energy for our day. The best way to support our body during the Energy Cycle is to eat plenty of fresh raw vegetables (such as a salad or juice), with a starch source (2 tbsp of cooked rice) to provide body with the energy it needs to maintain its natural biochemical balance.

The Regeneration Cycle

This Cycle Begins approximately 20:00 hours and ends at about 04:00 hours.

This is a crucial time for our body. All the "natural doctors" in our body wake up to meticulously work towards restoration. During this time our body is at work full force to heal and regenerate. This is why we need to get quality sleep. Our system works best when we are asleep. We need to allow our system to take over for its regeneration work by cooperating with deep sleep. During this cycle, the body assimilates all the foods that we consumed during the day and then processes the nutrients to regenerate the trillions of cells in our body. We need to have an undisrupted sleep for our body to effectively complete this cycle, otherwise, our system loses ability to regenerate cells. This on the other hand, will lead to their degeneration instead of regeneration. To avoid these adverse effects, we need to establish a consistent sleep pattern.

The Right Food

Each one of us differs from another. One specific assortment of food recommended by a specific nutritionist is not necessarily good for all. We need to understand our body, its activity level, our continuous affordability for a specific diet or supplement and geographical segmentation. We cannot put together a diet plan recommended by someone in Europe when we are in Asia. Food availability differs from region to region. Many elements come into play with our decisions when making food choices. As the saying goes, "one man's food is another man's poison", we need to experiment with food that is readily available to arrive at the right choice of food for our self. For assistance, do logon to www.tammmf.org.

Why most diets do not work?

One of the main reasons people have such a hard time losing weight and why we live in an obese society is that people are not eating their meals in a conscious state. We would have anxiously reviewed practically every diet plan ever written in the hope of shedding some weight. Not one of these diet plan mentions the state we need to be in, when eating. Eating is sacred and we need to respect the meticulous choice of food that we are to eat. Look at the food, concentrate on it and understand its functions once inside our body. Each variety of food will tell us a story. No diet plans has ever mentioned how important this is or even linked this to a cause of weight gain.

Sub-conscious State versus Conscious State

Sub-conscious state: Our sub-conscious state is what causes the "flight or fight" response which allows our body to adapt to stress or anxiety. In today's society, people are in a constant state of stress due to finances, raising a family, negative news stories, traffic, work pressures and many other things. When our body is in a sub-conscious state it continuously releases adrenalin into the bloodstream to deal with the stressful situation. Once the stress reaction is gone, it leaves the body exhausted and hungry. When the body is in a sub-conscious state, the digestive tract stops working and can even treat food as toxin. Our body is not designed to eat when we are in a "fight or flight" situation. It is designed to run or get away from the stressful situation. When people eat in a sub-conscious state, indigestion occurs as the digestive system is sluggish or shut down. Our system does not work properly and that leads to a poorly digested and assimilated meal. The ability to breakdown, absorb and process food is completely restricted which may cause weight gain, digestive disruption, upset stomach, gas, degenerative conditions, and even bloating.

Some examples of eating in a sub-conscious state are:

- Eating while in the car – whether driver or passenger
- Eating at our desk at work
- Eating while working on the computer
- Eating after a stressful work situation
- Eating while talking on the phone
- Eating while arguing with someone
- Eating while depressed or anxious
- Eating at a sporting event
- Eating while listening to the news on radio
- Eating while watching TV.

- Eating in a loud fast-food restaurant
- Eating while on stimulant prescription drugs.
- Eating when we are so hungry that we eat too fast.
- Eating fast because we are late for work, appointment etc.
- Eating while intoxicated
- Eating while listening to an argument
- Eating when angry
- Eating while walking
- Eating while lying down unless critically ill.
- Eating while having too much fun and partying

Conscious state: is the state responsible for relaxation, revitalization, repairing, healing, and recharging our body. When we are in a relaxed state or conscious state, our body is not dealing with stress. This state is able to break down, digest and absorb the vital components of the meals we eat. The fastest and easiest way to put our body in a conscious relaxed and responsive state is through deep breathing. Research has shown that deep breathing;

1) can almost instantly calm the body and mind and brings about clarity of thoughts,
2) detoxifies and releases toxins,
3) releases tension,
4) instantly relieves us of emotional problems,
5) relieves pain,
6) soothes our internal organs,
7) relaxes our muscles,
8) strengthens the immune system,
9) improves our posture,
10) improves quality of our blood,
11) Increases digestion fires for assimilation of food,
12) oxygenates our nervous system,
13) strengthens our lungs,
14) makes our heart stronger,
15) boosts energy level and improves stamina,
16) improves cellular regeneration
17) and elevates moods.

Many Eastern cultures have used this technique for thousands of years to reduce stress, prevent weight gain and achieve physiological balance within the body. Deep breathing can be done anywhere and anytime before meals to activate and support our digestive process. It should also be practiced after every stressful situation we encounter.

To Attain Conscious state before Meal

- Say grace – be thankful for the food.
- Perform a 2 minute breathing relaxation exercise. To relax our body before meals or during a stressful situation, find a quiet area to sit, close our eyes and take 9 deep breaths starting from deep in our belly all the way up through our upper lungs. Breathe in through our nose slowly until our lungs are fully inflated and then breathe out through our mouth until we push all the air out.

NOTE: People who have food allergies often eat in a subconscious state. This is because the body treats the food as toxin, allergen or threat and initiates an immune response toward the food. If suffering from food allergies start performing the deep breathing exercises before meals and thereafter, should start noticing better digestion and less allergic reactions within months.

Regimes to follow.....

- Avoid beverages with meals._Drinking water or any other beverages with meals dilutes the digestive juices, which slows down the digestion process. Water should be taken throughout the day and not with meals. Refrain from drinking coffee, milk, tea, juice, coca cola, carbonated drinks, energy drinks or any other beverage during meals or immediately after a meal.

- We can eat little meals throughout the day. This will actually help regulate our metabolism and keep our body clean. We are used to having elaborate meals as this is part of our culture. It might be difficult to change this as many of us have "teh-tarik" and "cup of coffee" friends. Little meals here represent, 1 apple, a fistful of roasted unsalted almond, 1 banana, a cup of carrots, a fistful of raisins, a cup of rice puffs etc

- Consciously chewing our food is just as important. We need to eat slowly and chew our food completely to a pulp before slowly swallowing it bit by bit. This process will allow our stomach to send a message to our brain, that we have had enough, so that we can avoid overeating and taking in excessive calories. We produce up to 32 ounces of saliva every day. Chewing our food will help our body absorb vital nutrients more thoroughly and rapidly due to the enzymes secreted in our saliva. After food is thoroughly chewed in the mouth, the tongue will recognize the various flavors of each food and then send messages to the brain, which in turn, orders production of the corresponding digestive juices that is needed to break down that food. Consciously chewing our food well, ultimately leads to more effective digestion and is also one of the best-kept secrets for losing weight.

~ The combination of food is as vital for health. Consuming organic foods grown in our own backyard is the best option. Our body depends on the correct balance of food types at each meal. It's important to observe and understand how the foods we eat react with one another once they are inside the body. Many competing and complicating theories exist about the best food or diet combination to follow regularly. We still have to depend on choices based on the biochemistry of our own body as each one of us differs from another. Some guidelines are given hereafter. Or logon to www.tammmf.org.

~ If possible, avoid eating proteins and starches in the same meal. When animal proteins and starches are combined and metabolized, the end product-results are normally acidic. At any time our body should be in a more alkaline state rather than acidic. Our gastric juices contain three enzymes that act on proteins, fats, and milk; they are pepsin, lipase, and rennin, respectively. Protein digestion requires an acidic environment initiated by the secretion of pepsin into the stomach. Pepsin splits the protein molecule to form hydrochloric acid. As the acidic level increases in the stomach while digesting protein, starch digestion ends. Optimum condition for protein digestion, excludes starch digestion. Starch digestion acts on its own by almost neutralizing the stomach acid, thus deactivating the enzymes and creating the climate for putrefaction and fermentation. Therefore only Non-starchy vegetables make for the best combinations with proteins.

Examples of unhealthy combinations of protein and starch:

Breakfast: Eggs, bacon, milk, sausage, or cheese combined with bread (muffins, bagels, waffles, and pancakes), or potatoes. Roti Prata, Chapati, Nasi lemak or Noodles with chicken, egg, mutton, beef, lentils or fish.

Lunch/Dinner: Red meat, white meat, eggs, fish or chicken combined with a baked potato, French fries, pasta, rice, chapatti, sandwich or bread.

Examples of healthy meals, is a combination of non starchy vegetable as listed hereafter;

Starchy Vegetables and Grains Not to be Combined With Protein: Beans, Bread, Corn, Lentils, Muffins, Pasta, Potatoes, Naan bread, Chapati, Roti prata, White Rice, Dosa, Idly, Yams, Sweet potatoes, Whole meal bread.

Non-Starchy Vegetables for Best Combination with Proteins: Alfalfa Sprouts, Bean sprouts, Asparagus, Bamboo Shoots, Broccoli, Cabbage, Carrots, Cauliflower, Celery, Eggplant, Green Beans, Leafy Lettuce, Leeks, Mushrooms, Okra, Onions, Peppers, Radishes, Sauerkraut (sengkuang), Snow Peas, Spinach, Water Chestnuts, Zucchini.

Unhealthy Example: Bread, Pasta, Rice, etc. + Any Acid Fruit or Fruit Juice

The digestion of carbohydrate begins in the mouth with an enzyme in our saliva called Ptyalin. Ptyalin, breaks down starch to maltose, which in turn further breaks down to dextrose in the intestines. Ptyalin from our saliva will not activate in a mildly acidic or strong alkaline environment. The acid in apple cider vinegar, oranges, lemons, salad dressings or any other fruits for that matter will completely stop the process of digestion, resulting in a poorly digested meal. Without the digestive enzymes, meals will likely ferment causing gas and producing toxic byproducts as well as decrease the absorption of nutrition from our meal.

Avoid Meat with Fruits or Fruit Juice.

Meat is protein. Meat is digested by an enzyme called Pepsin which will act favorably in an acidic environment. Therefore, we may think the addition of more acids, such as citrus fruits, might improve the digestive process. This is not so! Any additional acids like that of an orange, lemon or lime stops the secretion of the gastric juices necessary for protein digestion. Either the pepsin will not be secreted in the presence of another acid, or the acidic environment will destroy the pepsin. Any acid (including apple cider vinegar) on a salad, when eaten with a protein meal, stops the production of hydrochloric acid and interferes with protein digestion. But, there is an exception here; these acids can be combined with nuts and seeds. The high fat content of these foods will delay gastric secretion until the acids have been assimilated completely. Therefore, it is a better option to use raw (Yes. Only raw) nuts or seeds with salads to neutralize the acids always found in salad dressing.

We must avoid mixing milk, cheese and meat in the same meal. When two different types of high proteins are eaten together, the digestive secretions for one might stop the action of the other. In other words, our system gets confused and our body cannot correct or modify the digestive process to accommodate each food. Suppose milk was eaten with meat, this would initiate a highly acidic reaction and upset the proportions of lipase and pepsin acting on the meat from our meal. As a result, both proteins would not be fully digested, leading to indigestion and the development of toxins.

20% Acidic and 80% Alkaline

Our body is designed for alkaline foods - as much as possible. Our food composition should be 80% alkaline and 20% acidic. Alkaline foods aid in digestion, neutralizes acids, and helps restore the body's natural alkaline state. The foods shown in the Alkaline / Acidic chart should always be consumed fresh, juiced, raw, or lightly steamed and should be locally grown, preferably, organic too. Although some fruits are classified as acid fruits, once they are broken down in the body they convert the body fluids to an alkaline state.

The Cleansing Diet

Do not eat fruits after meals. Fruits should always be consumed on an empty stomach. For example, if we eat a slice of bread or rice and then some fruit, the fruit will be left in the stomach too long (as fruit is digested much faster) and cause the bread or rice to spoil thereby creating an acidic environment in our GI tract.

1. Eat fruits at least 20 minutes before meals for the fruit to move out of the stomach and into the small intestine before eating more food. When drinking fruit juice, make sure it is squeezed fresh and not from concentrates in a carton or can. When drinking fruit juice, hold it in our mouth for 10 seconds before swallowing to allow the enzymes in our mouth to work.

2. All fruit becomes alkaline in the body. When we eat fruit, benefits start right way, it keeps our body clean, nourishes our cells which directly means longevity.

3. A quick and easy way to start body cleansing and looking radiant is to do a **3-day Fruit fast**. Eat and drink fresh organic fruit and fresh juices for 3 days. We'll enjoy amazing results.

4. **Drinking ice cold water with meals should be avoided.** The water will solidify the oils (fats) in the meal which will slow digestion. As much as possible, do not drink water during a meal as digestion will be slowed. Proper and conscious chewing does not require us to drink water during meals. If we have to, it's best to sip room temperature water before or after meals. Cold water will also cause the body to expand excess energy to warm the water to body temperature. This additional process interferes with digestion.

5. **Wheat too is to be avoided:** The wheat we eat today is not the same as it was during our great grandparent's time. The wheat we eat today is actually more genetically modified in comparison to that which was

developed in the 60's and 70's. This toxic wheat contains a protein called gliadin which is an opiate that stimulates appetite and causes obesity.

6. **Avoid the following Gluten Containing Foods:** Pasta, cereal, grains, wheat, barley, white flour, wheat germ, wheat bran, bread, cakes, crackers, cookies, pastries, chips, vegetarian fish, hot dogs, burgers and fried foods. Replace with gluten free alternatives like, rice puffs, ragi, horse millet, mung dal, papadams, chick peas, oats etc.

7. **Avoid Drinking Packaged Milk:** Replace with natural alternatives such as coconut milk, almond milk or raw goat milk.

8. **Artificial Sweetener is to be avoided completely:** Artificial sweeteners are contained in diet sodas, many other diet products, and listed in many ingredient panels. The most dangerous sugar substitutes approved for consumer use are: saccharin, neotame, acesulfame potassium, and sucralose. Sucralose and aspartame are the most destructive to our body. Replace with natural sweeteners such as honey, stevia, or coconut or palm sugar.

9. **Refined Sugar and High Fructose Corn Syrup too is to be refrained from:** Carbonated sodas are one of the most common sources of refined sugars in the American diet. "Energy drink" and commercial fruit juices are no better. Avoid the following label ingredients: Corn syrup, Molasses, white sugar, dextrose, sorbitol, processed fructose and sucrose.

10. **Do away with refined Salt:** Refined salt (sodium chloride) is dangerous to consume considering its negative effects on the long run. It is refined and bleached and stripped of the vital minerals the body needs. It also contains additives that are harmful when ingested. Replace common refined salt with Himalayan Crystal Salt or Rock salt which is a healthier option. Our fore fathers never suffered from HBP even though they consumed lots of salty food. There were no refrigerators; therefore, meat and fish and almost everything that was in excess were soaked in salt water for preservation till a later date. They used the right salt and were healthier than all of us put together, who use refined salt.

11. **Stop using White Flour:** White flour is made from separating the bran from wheat, double bleaching it to change its color from yellow to white, adding synthetic vitamins, and increasing the amount of gluten the flour can produce. The synthetic vitamins that are added into the flour are toxic to the human body. Replace white flour with ragi.

12. **Avoid Soy Products:** Fresh soy milk and soybeans curd made at home is acceptable. But soy products as in vegetarian meals are high in Phytic acid which is damaging to the digestive tract and can block the absorption of nutrients and essential minerals like copper and calcium. These vegetarian meal makers are made to look like and taste like fish, chicken, mutton and many other non-vegetarian foods. Also, most mass production soy is genetically modified and contains pesticide residue. Fermented soy products, such as miso, tempeh, and tauchu, may be consumed in very small amount as it is known to have some benefits. However, soy product that is common in vegetarian meat substitutes are to be avoided. The problems with too much of this processed soy are: 91% of soy grown in this country is genetically modified – meaning it is chemically manipulated and loaded with pesticides. Most processed soy is industrially produced using hexane, which may lead to damage of the nervous system if consumed in very large quantities. Soy contains estrogen-like compounds called phytoestrogens. We sure do not need genetically modified hormones to be invading our body. Therefore, unless it's purely homemade with organic soybeans, it's best to keep away. We sure do not want to mess with our menstrual cycle, reproductive tract, the urinary tract, the heart and blood vessels, bones, breasts, skin, hair, mucous membranes, pelvic muscles, the brain many organ systems, including the musculoskeletal and cardiovascular systems and the brain – all of which are affected by estrogen.

13. **As Much as possible, Avoid Genetically Modified Foods:** The recombinant generic DNA technology changes the core genetic code of micro-organisms. Scientists use this genetic manipulation to create any trait they wish, or suppress natural traits they don't want. GMO foods are extremely damaging to the body.

14. **Microwave is super convenient but Micro waved Foods are harmful:** Using a microwave destroys and radiates all the nutrients in food and beverages. Use non toxic cookware for preparing foods instead.

15. **MSG (Monosodium Glutamate) or Aji-no-moto:** A manufactured food additive, MSG is used to enhance the flavor in foods. MSG is injected into lab animals to induce obesity, so we can only imagine what it does to our bodies. Since the introduction of MSG, diabetes has doubled and the obesity rates have skyrocketed. MSG is hidden in many ingredients such as spices, corn oil, frozen and canned foods, infant formulas, foods labeled "no added MSG", Cakes, cookies and even in cosmetics.

The Wonders of Spices

Every woman's dream is to be slim and beautiful. Every man's dream too is to be in shape and fit. For this dream to be fulfilled, we need to buy expensive packages at a popular gym and actually make time to show up every day. We need to follow an "out of the world" diet plan that might also cost us a bomb. Yet, this alone is not possible. Do not despair; get the spices in our kitchen to do the job for us….. Yes! Simply Spices…….

One amazing benefit of these herbs is that they're very low in calories, while being dense in vitamins and minerals. In our body, they're thermogenic, meaning they naturally support our metabolism to help us burn calories. We feel satisfied more easily, so we tend to eat less. Studies show that consuming certain spices before each meal can potentially reduce our caloric intake.

Due to their nutrient-dense status, they promote our overall well-being with antioxidants more potent than many fruits and vegetables. Herbs and spices promote health and well-being in our entire body and not just in a particular area. This "whole person" approach is why we believe these spices and herbs can benefit our health so greatly.

Cinnamon – considered the best spice for dieters. Only a ¼ tsp of cinnamon is needed to improve our carbohydrate metabolism twenty folds. Cinnamon is known to control sugar level in our blood. Sugar as we know, is ravenous and is known for all the jumps and wakes in diabetes. Even the smell of cinnamon can trick our appetite and give the illusion of saturation. Cinnamon can be added to tea, coffee, yogurt, baked apple, pumpkin and whole lot of foods.

Cayenne pepper (yes! Dried red chili powder) – We need to hand pick these red chilies, sun-dry and mill to fine powder. Just a pinch of this pepper added to the dish, accelerates metabolism by 25 percent, reduces blood sugar levels and suppresses appetite. People with gastrointestinal ailments need to administer gradually with turmeric.

Turmeric – is considered the grandmother of all spices because its benefits are so amazing and far-reaching. This is a popular Indian seasoning and tops the list in Naturopathy. This spice is an excellent antioxidant and activator of metabolism. Its unique compound curcumin contained in this spice provides us with these "whole-person" benefits. It prevents the accumulation of body fat, improves digestion, supports healthy joint functions, promotes radiant skin and so much more…………...

Cardamom - Spicy and burning spice from India. This spice, first of all, is an excellent antioxidant and fat burner. Cardamom splits and displays cholesterol, boosts immunity and fights depression. It can be added to almost all dishes. Cardamom is a great source of mineral manganese. Manganese is the key to production of an enzyme that scavenges and destroys free radicals. Apart from that, cardamom also has very strong detoxifying properties that help to cleanse the body and protect it from diseases like cancer.

Anise - Excellent spice that lowers appetite. The amazing properties and benefits of this plant have been known since the time of Hippocrates, and Avicenna. For example, ancient Greek athletes were always chewing anise seeds to suppress hunger and not to fill the stomach before responsible contests. Besides anise has an uplifting aroma that soothes and gives fresh breath. Anise is well known as a carminative and an expectorant. Its ability to decrease bloating and settle the digestive tract still is used today, especially in pediatrics. In high doses, it is used as an antispasmodic and an antiseptic and for the treatment of cough, asthma, and bronchitis.

Ginger - is our faithful assistant in well being and weight loss. Ginger is considered one of the world's best foods. It will give our dishes a wonderful flavor, and we also improve the digestive system, will speed up the metabolism and reduce the level of cholesterol in the blood. Ginger improves the absorption of essential nutrients in the body by stimulating gastric and pancreatic enzyme secretion. Ginger combat stomach discomfort and is ideal in assisting digestion thereby improving food absorption. Ginger is known in Naturopathy to reduce inflammation in a similar way as aspirin and ibuprofen.

Black pepper - can be found in almost every kitchen. It is also one of the world's best foods. Because it's a common spice, we are unaware of its beneficial properties. Black pepper can destroy fat cells and burn extra calories, improves brain and nervous system.

Black pepper stimulates the taste buds in such a way that an alert is sent to the stomach to increase hydrochloric acid secretion, thereby improving digestion. Hydrochloric acid is necessary for the digestion of proteins and other food components in the stomach. When the body's production of hydrochloric acid is insufficient, food may sit in the stomach for an extended period of time, leading to heartburn or indigestion, or it may pass into the intestines, where it can be used as a food source for unfriendly gut bacteria, which produces gas and irritation resulting in diarrhea or constipation.

Black pepper has long been recognized as a *carminitive*, (a substance that helps prevent the formation of intestinal gas), a property likely necessary due to its beneficial effect of stimulating hydrochloric acid production. In addition, black pepper has *diaphoretic* (promotes sweating), and *diuretic* (promotes urination) properties.

Black pepper has demonstrated impressive antioxidant and antibacterial effects-yet another way in which this wonderful seasoning promotes the health of the digestive tract. And not only does black pepper help us derive the most benefit from our food, the outer layer of the peppercorn stimulates the breakdown of fat cells, keeping us slim while giving us energy to burn.

Naturopathy Post Partum (Confinement) Diet

It's best if a care-giver is assigned for the mother and baby for 40 days (or longer). The mother needs to rest and spend her time bonding with the new member of the family.

- Create a food schedule for friends and nearby family, who are willing to bring mom yummy and easy to digest foods every day. Otherwise, we'll end up having lots of prohibited food due to ignorance.

- Naturopathy emphasizes mainly on the proper diet regime during this time, to ensure the health of both baby and mother. Foods need to be fresh, not processed, served warmed, very soupy and moist in consistency.

- Make sure that the dishes prepared include digestive spices, such as cumin, caraway, ginger, mustard seed, clove, basil, turmeric, fenugreek, cinnamon and garlic (roasted only).

- Avoid eating red meat for at least two weeks or 40 days if possible. Soup stocks are okay. Do not binge on caffeine, white sugar, raw vegetables' dry, crunchy foods, too many varieties of beans (including tofu) and too many eggs.

- Make sure mother and baby are warm, oily, and feeling loved. This would mean that a person should be appointed to massage the twosome with sesame oil, daily. Use lots of sesame oil, olive oil or ghee internally. The best bet would be to let the mother and child stay warm indoors.

- Most importantly, assure mom that it is okay for her to take this time to receive unconditional love and support, no matter how awkward it may feel for her. Make her feel special, loved and cared for. Not for a moment, she is to feel neglected or rejected as it will affect her overall recovery.

- **Enjoy these important "Secrets" for the first 40 days after childbirth.**

  After the delivery of a baby, the digestive power is often weakened; a new mother's digestive system is very delicate. Yet her nutritional needs are great. Choice of foods and how well a mother digests her food has a great deal to do with the quality of her nursing the baby, avoiding depression and colic, and the quality of mom's rejuvenation, strength, comfort, and resulting spontaneous and natural expression of mothering. The following suggestions are time tested, from the ancient system of natural health care called Naturopathy, and found common to many cultures around the world.

- *Preferred Foods*

  Pure water, warm, oily, soupy or moist, nourishing, delicious, often mushy or creamy textured, gentle on the digestion of foods. Seasoning to support digestion too – include ginger, black (not chili) pepper, roasted/sautéed not raw garlic. Fresh ingredients, freshly prepared by a happy cook – these have the best life force. Use ample oiliness, seasonings, moisture, warmth, and of course, love. Mom and Baby will feel the benefits.

- **There are lots of yummy things we can do with this list**. It's good to make a list of all that can be eaten and cannot be eaten and have it pinned on our refrigerator. Have a list of the preferred vegetables, seasonings, grains, sweets and proteins. Please, please.... avoid making enough for the next day. Leftovers become guaranteed gas for mom and baby. Use of unusually generous good fats, especially clarified butter, ghee and sesame oil cannot be over-emphasized, unless with gall bladder/liver related medical issues.

- **We need all six tastes** in our main meals for balanced nutrition. These herbs and spices help digestion, deliciousness and rejuvenation - often lactation as well. We lean more on the sweet, fresh, sour, and salty tastes throughout the 40 days. For the right range of herbs and spices during confinement, logon to www.tammmf.org.

- **Proteins** are boiled warm milk, milk puddings without egg; split hulled mung beans in thin soup, perhaps chick peas soaked overnight and well-cooked. Legumes combined with grains, nuts or seeds give a complete amino acid complement. Almond or other milky nut that are nourishing must be well soaked, (24 - 48 hours) for snack, or prepared with nut milks, soups, vegetables, grains, or sauces. Lassi, a curd or buttermilk drink thinned half with water and seasoned, sweet or savory after 21 days is preferred. Any type of cheese and other unfermented cheeses to be given only after 3 weeks; rarely does tofu or fermented cheeses work; most mothers and their babies have digestion trouble with soy - and the hard cheeses. Red meat and fish soups after about 4 weeks for non-vegetarians.

- **Carbs**- Basmati is the best (cook with extra ½-1 cup water per cup of rice), pastas, tapioca, yams, oats, quinoa and Ragi. Mothers who have been eating brown rice must refrain from eating it as it is rougher on tender bowels. Favor less refined sugars – instead use especially the iron rich ones like date, dark Indian Jaggery, unrefined, molasses if possible. Do not cook with honey. Moms need extra carbs including healthy sweets, even if unable to breastfeed, it is needed for rebuilding.

- **Fruits** include dried iron rich fruits (soaked or stewed) for strength and muscle building, sweet fresh (not chilled) and freshly squeezed sweet fruit juices (for their life force and gentle cleansing). Most fruit ferments, is not to be taken alone. Dates are excellent. Papaya is excellent and also aids digestion. Coconut milk is soothing and delicious in puddings, cream sauces, soups, smoothies and when combined with fruit and baked food. Add ginger, lots of it. It creates warmth.

- **Seasonings are very important** – but never with Aji-no-moto (MSG), refined salt or any other short-cut seasoning. Use instead, Fennel, Fenugreek, Basil, Cumin, Caraway; Fresh Garlic - prepared only by roasting or mincing and browning in oil or butter; these also help lactation. Cardamom, Clove, Cinnamon, Ginger (fresh is usually best), Turmeric, pinches of hing (Asafoetida) Hingvastika or roasted

Asafoetida, Lime, Orange or Lemon juice and Peel, Black Pepper, Paprika, Pippali, a little Black Mustard Seed, Tamarind, Marjoram, Thyme, Oregano, Tarragon, Licorice Powder, Ajwan. During the first week, use extra ginger, garlic, pepper, pippali, cardamom, and clove. Leave onions out during confinement.

- **Vegetables** – Contrary to health experts, Food has to be cooked until tender to minimize gas, also with "oil" or butter and seasoned well – Asparagus, beet, carrot, fresh fenugreek leaves, pumpkin, okra, some green beans or broccoli well seasoned if she is not of thin body type, and peeled eggplant and kale, spinach, or chard may also be fine after 2-3 weeks. Be sure to use oiliness, seasonings, salt, and lime or lemon juice with all the meals.

- **Fats** - Use healthy fats and oils more abundantly than normal. This is important for postnatal hormonal, lubricating, cleansing and rejuvenation needs. Emphasize clarified butter and ghee, sesame and toasted sesame oils, butter, coconut oil and spice it well, some olive is good too. Note: clarified butter (ghee), coconut, and a little sesame are the best for cooking healthy.

- ***Do Away with all these food during confinement***

  Dry, cold, rough, hard to digest, heavy, clogging, fermented foods, and sharp pungent food may, for various reasons aggravate mother's or infant's digestion, accumulate into colic, or slow mom's rejuvenation. Some are bigger no-nos than others. Rushed or irritated atmosphere in cooking, serving, and eating also weakens digestion, hence Mom-baby discomforts creeps in.

- A Big "No" to - Coffee, sodas, chocolate, alcohol, garlic (dry, raw, or undercooked), onion, radish, chilies and the cabbage family is to be avoided.

- Chilled Foods and Drinks – like ice cream, salads, and chilled foods/drinks in general. If Mom needs to cool down a little, or experiencing hot flashing, prepare room temperature drink with fennel, coriander, cumin, a little mint, chamomile, ginger and essential oils.

- Tough/Heavy food - include red meats, fermented cheeses; cold temp, homogenized, pasteurized, lots of nuts, sour cream, yogurt, eggs, fried foods (sauté is good, seals nutrients), canned, preserved and fermented fruits or vegetable to be avoided.

- Dried or drying foods – Rule here is those foods obviously pulling moisture from system to digest, like dried fruits, crackers, toast, even sweet and white potatoes are to be avoided. Instead, balance with oil, moisture, sweet, sour, salty tastes and hydrating influences at best. Rough dryer grains (millet, brown rice, corn, buckwheat, sometimes as mush) can be unsatisfying to fragile innards. Reduce drying, bitter, and astringent herbs, and watch out for the legumes - heavy wind producers. 2 – 3 cups of strong Sage or Turmeric tea is used by midwives to dry up lactation. Avoid fruit-vegetable mixed powders.

- Tomatoes, Peas, Peppers, Sprouts, Salads. Go easy also on dark Leafy Greens first couple of weeks. Keep away from other bitter/astringent foods. The greens are so high in iron and bone flexibility minerals, (especially the stems for the latter), and magnesium, if they sound good to Mom, balance with oiliness, generous ginger or roasted garlic or hing, salt, fennel or cumin or caraway or dill, and perhaps a squeeze of lime, and some sweeter vegetable or a pinch of raw sugar as well.

- Fermented Foods – Yes, includes easy or hard-to-digest foods, plus leftovers, after 6 hours or so, because of rapid rejuvenation needs and these have more degenerative energy. Fermented food such as Soy Sauce, Vinegar, Pickles, Tempeh, Miso, most Cheeses and Mushrooms. Make enough food for just lunch and cook again for dinner.

- Hydrogenated or most cooked vegetable oils (due to trans-fatty acids). And we get to forget the low-fat idea, for health, emotional, hormonal, mental and physical reasons, unless medically advised otherwise (such as from liver damage, alcohol or gall bladder problems).

- Cooking with Honey is proven to create toxic accumulations over time in the body channels, and around nerves. It is one of the most difficult toxin to remove! Raw or with drinkable warmth is fine.

- Leavenings – Yeast, Baking Powder and all Soda are somewhat of a strain on Mom and Baby too. This includes thosai, idlies and sweet apom.

Meals honoring these principles are a great gift for the Mom and her new baby. Mom and baby will nurture an inevitable bonding and spend quiet time on restoration work during this time which will have such long lasting effect on their quality of health and family life. And also the life of all involved too. So these little adjustments can make a really big difference at this time and with long lasting impact too – "*40 days confinement care is equivalent to 40 years of healthy life.*" *says our great gurus!*

The Wonders of Eggs

Many of us are either refraining from eating eggs, limiting intake or have completely stopped eating it. First and foremost, contrary to the popular myth, eggs do not cause heart disease. As a matter of fact, there was never any evidence that linked heart diseases to eggs. More so, eggs do not even raise our blood cholesterol. Of course, eggs contain cholesterol but the developing embryo in the egg needs it to produce sex hormones – but then again, we too....... need it.

Eggs are 100% complete food. The yolks of eggs contain all of the necessary fat-soluble vitamins (A, D, E, and K), iron, and heart-healthy omega-3 fat that are important in our diet. The whites of eggs too have all the water-soluble B vitamins. Either cooked, half cooked or raw, eggs are the highest-quality complete protein on this planet. It has all the amino acids we need in exactly the ratios we need. Simply put, an Egg has enough substance to produce life, therefore it can NEVER be harmful to us.

Raw eggs are even better as it's an excellent source of essential fatty acid DHA (docosahexaenoic acid), which is known to ease hypertension, problems with brain function, heart disease, arthritis, diabetes, and also stimulates mental alertness. Unfortunately, DHA (and some nutrients and some proteins) collapses in the cooking process.

People stopped eating raw eggs because of a hype that it contains salmonella bacteria which is poisoning. But there has never been a known incident that it came from eggs. Raw eggs are very safe to eat. We can absorb a raw egg in as little as 30 minutes while it takes 2 to 4 hours to digest a cooked egg. Adding raw egg into our diet is easy, just add it in a protein shake and drink up. We will not even taste the difference. If we need to eat it raw or any other way, just think of it as oyster.

All Ill Effects of Eggs Are Eggs-Xaggerated

Eggs have gotten a bad reputation because the yolks are high in cholesterol. Each egg contains approximately 180mg to 190mg of cholesterol, which is 60% to 70 % of the recommended daily intake. Many of us believe that if we ate eggs, it would raise cholesterol in our blood and contribute to heart diseases. This is not so, in fact the more cholesterol we eat, the less our body (liver) produces.

Our body has the ability to regulate cholesterol. Cholesterol is often seen as a negative word, the moment it is mentioned, we automatically relate it to heart diseases, medication and many other health complications. Some of us even declare that we do not want to die young and avoid eggs. How can we die eating eggs? An egg has all the nutrients needed to transform a single cell into an entire chicken. It has a life inside it and how can we die with eating life? Eggs are so fragile and it is packed with all the necessary nutrients to give us a whole chick – brain, eyes, nervous system, skeletal system, muscles, feathers and claws. All we have to do is keep it warm to hatch - and no fertilization or watering is needed. How can this be bad for us? Egg is the only form of complete food on the face of this earth.

Cholesterol is a structural molecule that is an essential part of every single cell membrane in our body. It plays an important role in the making of steroid hormones like testosterone and estrogen. Without cholesterol we will not exist. It's incredibly important for life and our body has evolved in elaborate ways to ensure that we always have enough of it available to sustain life. Our liver produces enough of it.

There is nothing backing the recommendation of 2 to 3 eggs a week. There isn't really any scientific support for these limitations. We can eat eggs in all our meals and nothing drastic is known to have happened.

It's the most available potent protein food for anyone – babies weaning away from milk, young students, matured students, working adults, elderly persons, ailing patients and people recuperating from diseases.

To avoid any possible problem with raw eggs:

(1)   Eat only cage-free, hormone-free eggs,
(2)   Do not eat the egg if the shell is cracked,
(3)   Do not eat the egg if it smells foul and
(4)   Eat only eggs that have a gel-like white and a firm, round yolk.

To avoid any possible problems with cooked eggs;

(1)   Do not scramble eggs with trans-fats,
(2)   As much as possible, eat eggs cooked at home, except for hard boiled or half boiled eggs. (Restaurateurs use re-cycled oil or trans-fats),

More egg-xcellent egg benefits

(1)   Eggs are excellent food for just about anyone.
(2)   Eggs can be prepared in minutes – the best fast food ever.
(3)   Eggs are not the cause for elevation in blood cholesterol.
(4)   Eggs do not clog up the coronary vessels.
(5)   Eggs are low in calories, great for caloric restriction diets.
(6)   Eggs have a very high nitrogen-retention value. Hence it is extremely useful in post-surgical care, trauma, and in post-management of hypo-volemic shock against negative nitrogen balance. (A negative Nitrogen balance can be construed as a clinical evaluation of malnutrition).

(7) Eggs contain vitamin D in its most natural form.

(8) Eggs are known to protect against fatty liver.

(9) Eggs are very rich in methionine – a sulfur-containing amino acid that is very crucial in blocking damaging free radicals.

(10) Eggs are excellent for healthy growth of hair, nails and skin.

(11) Eggs are great for our eyes - macular degeneration (degeneration of the macula area of the retina in the eyes. This is responsible for central vision for reading, and detailed vision), edema (water retention), and various skin lesions. It contains nutrients that are more readily available to our body compared to any other sources.

(12) Eggs lower our risk of developing cataracts.

(13) Egg yolk contains choline - a significant nutrient that helps regulate the brain functions, cardio and nervous system.

(14) Eggs contain the right kind of fat.

(15) Two eggs a day improve our lipid profile. Research suggests that it is saturated fat that is used to cook the egg that raises cholesterol rather than dietary cholesterol in the egg.

(16) Eggs contain all the 9 essential amino acids

Eggs are sooooooooo Important……..

There are 22 biologically active amino acids in our body. Although there are more than 100 found, our body uses only 22 of them. Amino acids are the building blocks of protein. There are essential and non-essential amino acids. Essential amino acids are the ones that is "essential" in our diet and non-essentials are the ones produced by our body. Our body cannot create essential amino acids with our own metabolism. We need to acquire them through foods containing them.

Essential amino acids vs. non-essential amino acids

"Essential" does not mean necessary, but rather, that the 9 essential amino acids must be acquired through food. "Non-essential" means that our body can produce the amino acids on its own, without dietary supplementation.

Sometimes our body is deficient in its ability to make amino acids, and in severe cases it can cause diseases or health problems. Therefore, we need to supply our body with the 9 essential amino acids from the food we eat consistently, and assist our body to produce the amino acids it needs to survive, and indeed, thrive!

Amino acids are vital to every part of human function. 75% of the human body is made up of amino acids. One of the most important properties of amino acids is that it assists in muscle building. Amino acids are boasted as the key ingredients in many body-building supplements. However, the one problem with amino acids is that it deteriorates. Our body stores extra starch and protein as fat, to use later. Amino acids are not stored, but they can be replaced. We need to replenish amino acids with constant consumption of food on a daily basis as foods with amino acids are the building blocks of protein. Amino acids are responsible for strength, repair and rebuilding that happen inside our body. Our tissues, our cells, our enzymes and our brain all get their nourishment and protection from amino acids.

Essential Amino acids	Non-Essential Amino acids
Histidine	Alanine
Isoleucine	Arginine
Leucine	Aspartic Acid
Lysine	Cysteine
Methionine	Glutamis Acid
Phenylalanine	Glutamine
Threonine	Glycine
Tryptophan	Proline
Valine	Serine
	Tyrosine
	Asparagine
	Selenocysteine

Recommended daily Amounts of Amino Acids

The estimations are just a guide. This chart is to show that eggs are a near-perfect source of protein, whether eaten whole, raw, half cooked, poached or cooked in any which way that we prefer, contains all 9 essential amino acids and 12 non-essential amino acids combined, period.

Amino Acid(s)	Mg per Kg Body Weight	Food Sources
Histidine	10	Eggs, Sesame, Parmesan, Peanuts
Isoleucine	20	Eggs, White fish, Tofu, Parmesan, Pork
Leucine	39	Eggs, Sesame, Parmesan, White fish
Lysine	30	Eggs, Parmesan, White fish
Methionine	15	Eggs, Sesame, White fish, Nuts, Mustardseeds
Phenylalanine	25	Eggs, Sesame, Whitefish, Peanuts, Parmesan
Threonine	15	Eggs, Sesame, Whitefish, Smelts
Tryptophan	4	Eggs, Sesame, Winged beans, Chia seeds
Valine	26	Eggs, Sesame, Parmesan, Red Meat

Eggs are the only form of protein that is jam-packed with all 9 essential amino acids and 12 non essential amino acids required for our health.

White Bread is Convenient Food but NOT Good Food

White Bread has become compulsory in every household. White Bread is readily available from hypermarkets to convenient stores 24/7. Working moms, housewives, working women, and bachelors are completely at rest because they know that bread comes to their rescue all the time. Bread has become an obvious part of our daily meal which we enjoy eating, least realizing the ill effects that we are gradually acquiring from it. It's not only that white bread isn't good for our health; it can actually be a real set-back to our health.

Bread does not contain the original vitamins found in grains, only imitations. White bread is enriched with synthetic vitamins. Evidently, white bread is dead bread. Of course the labels say that the bread is made with "enriched" flour. Do we really know what "enriched" means? Why is color of bread is so white when the flour is made of wheat which is brown? It's because the flour used to make bread is chemically bleached, just like how we bleach our white bed-sheets. So what does "enrich" here means"? When we eat white bread, we are also eating residual chemical bleach.

Good Nutrition is never found in white bread. All nutritious values are lost in the process of making flour white. Most of the good unsaturated fatty acids, that are high in food value, are lost in the milling process alone, and almost all the vitamin E is lost with the removal of wheat germ and bran. As a result, the remaining flour contained in the white bread we buy has only poor quality proteins and redundant fattening starch. But that is not the whole bread story as to the loss of nutrients. Our bread is fortified with the cheapest form of minerals and vitamins that are poorly absorbed by our body. That too only a small fraction of what is lost is replaced just for label sake.

Different Flour mills use different chemical bleaches, all of which are very bad for our health in the long run. Some of the chemicals used are: Oxide of nitrogen, chlorine, chloride, nitrosyl and benzoyl peroxide. These chemicals are mixed with various chemical salts. One particular bleaching agent, chloride oxide, combined with whatever proteins that are still left in the flour produce alloxan. Alloxon is a chemical that is used to produce diabetes in laboratory animals. Chlorine oxide on the other hand, destroys the vital wheat germ oil.

Horrific numbers from a statistic study run by the university of California, shows huge loss of nutrients when white bread is made: About 50% of all calcium is lost, 70% of phosphorus, 80% of iron, 98% of magnesium, 75% of manganese, 50% of potassium and 65% of copper is destroyed when white bread is made, 80% of thiamin, 60% of riboflavin, 75% of niacin, and 50% of pantothenic acid. So it is obvious that white bread should be avoided. Whole wheat, rye and grain breads made with whole wheat flour are a better option. It is also good to always read the labels and never buy bread or foods that contain artificial flavors, colors, bleached flour, preservatives, hydrogenated or partially hydrogenated oils.

We need a mucus balance in our body. Mucus is needed to bind toxic acids and remove them from our body. If not for this protective mucus lining, the acid would burn through the cells and tissues of our organs. Eating acidic food leads to mucus build up as well; causing indigestion, nasal and lung congestion as in Asthma and continuous throat clearing is required. All white flour has high level of gluten in it and therefore, white bread is high in gluten content. Gluten is active in mucus forming.

Too much mucus thickens the lining of our colon, glues up kidneys and other organs causing congestion in our system. The trouble is in the name itself, Glue – ten (to be understood as Glue to the power of ten). When colon and other internal organs get glued up, nutrients cannot be absorbed and toxins cannot be expelled. The bowel flora becomes disrupted and the body loses its natural ability to cleanse and heal.

White flour is reputed as the number one enemy in nutrition. White bread, an enhanced version cannot be better. Consistent white bread meals are very challenging for our body. There is no dietary fibre whatsoever in white bread. The next time we stop by to buy bread, take a few seconds and imagine acidic, toxicities, mucus forming fat attack taking place inside of us.

The Deadly Kitchen Assistant

We know that raw plant foods contain more nutrients than cooked foods. The vitamins and phyto-nutrients (plant-based nutrients) from vegetables are very fragile and can be easily destroyed by heat. We know that half cooked, blanched or steamed vegetables retain its nutritional values and is more bio-available compared to overcooked food. But it did not occur to us that beneficial Carotenoids, antioxidants and other important nutritional molecules are all easily and instantly destroyed by microwave energy?

Microwaves destroy our food at a cellular level. It destroys all vital nutrients in food. We are bound to suffer nutritional deficiencies with micro-waved meals. Microwave absolutely extinguishes the nutritional value of our food, destroying the very vitamins and phyto-nutrients needed to prevent disease and support good health. Studies have shown that as much as 98% of nutrients are destroyed by microwaving.

Microwaving a meal is the worst way to cook our foods. What happens during the process is that the microwave excites the water molecules inside whatever we are cooking. This causes heat to be formed from the inside out and results in a cell-by-cell "destruction" of the food especially, vegetable, causing total decomposition of the vitamins and phyto-nutrients. We will now have an excellent disease promoting meal.

Micro-waved food can be considered "dead" food. Our food gets molecularly destroyed at every level. The entire range of vitamins and phyto-nutrients content is destroyed.

Anyone who says microwaving food is a healthy way to cook is totally ignorant of nutrition and healthy cooking methods. Micro-waved meals tends to look appetizing but don't be fooled by appearances. What's really deceptive about microwave cooking is that the food still appears to be basically the same, but at the cellular level, it's like a nuclear war has taken place. The actual molecular structure has been destroyed. If we could see micro-waved foods with a high powered microscope, we'd never eat them again because we would recognize just what a nutritional waste-yard our food has really become.

If we continuously cook our meals in a convenient microwave oven, we will inevitably suffer chronic nutritional deficiencies that promote diseases and many other health problems.

Symptoms of chronic nutritional deficiencies in the Swiss, Russian and German scientific clinical studies show that:

- Continually eating food processed from a microwave oven causes long term - permanent - brain damage by 'shorting out' electrical impulses in the brain by de-polarizing or de-magnetizing the brain tissue.
- The human body cannot metabolize or break down the unknown by-products created in micro-waved food.
- Male and female hormone production is shut down and/or altered by continually eating micro-waved foods.
- The effects of micro-waved food by-products are long term or permanently residual within the human body.
- Minerals, vitamins, and nutrients of all micro-waved food is reduced or altered so that the human body gets little or no benefit, or the human body absorbs altered compounds that cannot be broken down.
- The minerals in vegetables are altered into cancerous, free radicals when cooked in microwave ovens.
- Micro-waved foods cause stomach and intestinal cancerous growths and tumors. This may explain the rapidly increased rate of colon cancer.
- The prolonged eating of micro-waved foods causes cancerous cells to increase in human blood.
- Continual ingestion of micro-waved food causes immune system deficiencies through lymph gland and blood serum alterations.
- Eating micro-waved food causes loss of memory, concentration, emotional instability, and a decrease of intelligence.
- Microwaving emits +ions.

The Apple Magic

"An APPLE a day keeps the DOCTOR Away" – this is so true.

The most popular of all fruits are apples. Apples are fruits that we have known for generations although it is not in our list of tropical fruits. Apples have been present in the mythology and religions of many cultures. Though they not locally grown and harvested, apples are readily and conveniently available anytime and anywhere. It's an all season fruit. There isn't anyone who does not know an apple. Every one of us has gone pass the "A for apple" stage in our life. Apple is indeed an "A" class fruit.

Apple is magic food. Apples are everyone's all time favorite fruit. Apples are known to help during recuperation of illnesses. This is why many visitors in hospitals bring a bag of apples for their ailing friends.

Most fruits contain a compound called pectin but apples contain very high concentrations of this compound. It is the white stuff under the skin of apples.

Primarily, Pectin is used as a treatment for digestive disorders. Pectin is high in fiber and is helpful in regulating bowel movements. One suffering from diarrhea may take apple pectin to firm the stool and reduce some of the inflammation associated with loose stool. Conversely, apple pectin also helps in bowel movements for people experiencing constipation. Regular consumption of apples helps with digestive problems, regulates our bowels and prevents flare-ups. Apple pectin is also helpful for people with colitis, irritable bowel disease, and other digestive disorders.

High fiber in apples tends to increase activity in the intestines, which can provide numerous benefits. Apples are a low cost way of managing intestinal conditions.

Pectin is also an antioxidant. Antioxidant foods confer numerous health benefits, including lowering cholesterol, in managing diabetes, and potentially reducing the risks of other subsequent diseases. Since Pectin is found in apples, it makes it easier for us to access and integrate it into the diet.

The benefits of pectin from apples especially in maintaining our health generally are endless. Apples can be eaten by people of all ages and with all levels of health conditions.

Health benefits of apple

1) Apple is notable for its impressive list of phyto-nutrients, and anti-oxidants. Too many studies suggest that its components are essential for normal growth, development and overall well-being.

2) Apples are low in calories; 100gm of apples provide only 50 calories. Apples contain no saturated fats or cholesterol and are rich in dietary fiber, which helps prevent absorption of dietary-LDL or bad cholesterol in the gut. The fiber in apple also saves our colon's mucous membrane from exposure to toxic substances by binding toxic chemicals inside the gut and ferrying them out of the body.

(3) Apples are naturally rich in antioxidant and phyto nutrients called *flavonoids* and *polyphenolics*. These compounds help the body protect from damaging effects of free radicals.

(4) Apples contain good quantities of *vitamin-C* and *beta-carotene*. As we know, Vitamin C is a powerful natural antioxidant. Consistent consumption of foods rich in vitamin C helps the body develop resistance against infectious agents, scavenging and harmful, pro-inflammatory free radicals from the body.

(5) Apples are a good source of B-complex vitamins such as riboflavin, thiamin, and pyridoxine (vitamin B-6). These vitamins come as assisting factors for enzymes in metabolism as well as in synthetic functions that takes place inside our body.

(6) Apple contains minerals like potassium, phosphorus, and calcium. Potassium is an important factor in cells and body fluids that helps in regulating heart rate and blood pressure; thus, counters the bad influences of sodium.

(7) Apples raise good cholesterol, lowers bad cholesterol and contributes to weight loss.

Cholesterol is manufactured in the liver. Statin drugs, such as Lipitor and Crestor, reduce cholesterol very effectively. These drugs block an enzyme in our liver from making cholesterol. Now this is what we call, interference with the natural processes of our body. The problem is that statins can be hard on the liver, which is why people who take them must have a blood test done periodically to make sure their liver is not becoming irritated and inflamed.

The liver is one of the largest organs in the body. It functions even if only 50 percent of it is healthy. We will not be able to see an abnormality in our blood unless we do substantial damage to our liver. Drugs have their limitations besides side effects. Even if we are on medications, we are asked by our doctors to check our liver enzymes. Now, why do need to check our liver enzymes, when we are given medications to improve our condition? This can only mean two things; 1) they are unsure of our condition and are running a test on us or, 2) the medication is not working.

Caring for our liver is our responsibility. Let's start by eating apples. Eat apples as they are, along with their peel in order to get maximum health-benefits. Two apples a day reduce LDL cholesterol so effectively. Besides acquiring substantial health benefits from apples, we do not do any detrimental harm to our liver. Try it to know it!

Neeragaram

Left-over rice soaked overnight – excellent food

During the agricultural revolution, the farmers had to leave for work at the farm in the wee hours of the morning. There was no special practice of breakfast as we do now in current times. The first meal for a typical South Indian family was previous day's cooked rice that was mushed with plain water and soaked overnight in an earthen pot. This rice mixture was consumed with some buttermilk, salt, onions, garlic, green chilies, pepper corns, fennels, cumin and ginger with a little portion of gooseberry or lemon pickle. This was considered the best food to prepare oneself for physical labor although its nutritious values were not understood then.

While fermenting left over rice, no starter microbial cultures are added and as a result all varieties of bacteria grow in it. There are also the good ones that feed on the rice nutrients and secrete vitamin B12. It is a known fact that vitamin B12 rich food prevents anemia, fatigue and tiredness. As such, people who indulge in laborious activities are bound to benefit from the intake of vitamin B12 and several other micronutrients by eating this soaked rice.

For centuries, this has been the staple food of many South Indian families, particularly of the low income groups. Neeragaram is found to be a very compact and complete breakfast. It has the rare B6 and B12 vitamins which are not easily available from other food. During the fermentation process, the rice generates and harbors trillions of beneficial bacteria that eases digestion and has many disease fighting and immunity strengthening agents. It safeguards our defense system and keeps them battle-ground fit and ready to defend us from diseases

Most systems of modern medicines and nutrition usually frown at the thought of stale, flavorless and tasteless food. We insist on eating freshly prepared food for good health. However, this stale food dish seems to be an exception. For the poor, it's a thing that is helpful and beneficial. Leftover rice is made good use without wastage. And fermentation enhances its nutritional health giving capabilities making it an appropriate breakfast. Farmers who take this can work for hours without feeling hungry, in the scorching heat of the midday sun with full zest and energy.

For more info, please logon to: www.tammmf.org.

Homemade Curd is Way Better than milk

Curd is a dairy product which provides innumerable nutritional values and health benefits. Curd is generously used in many cuisines as it improves taste when used in the preparation of other food items. When curd is flavored, modified, improved, fortified, processed or transformed from its original form, its yogurt. The ones we find at our grocers.

Dairy products are regarded as an important part in the diet of human beings. And curd is one such product. Curd is prepared by fermentation of milk. Simply boil some milk, let it cool completely, mix in some natural yogurt and let it stand overnight. Result: we have curd that provides more nutritional values than milk.

Nutritional and health benefits of curd

- Improve the digestive system
- Strengthen the immune system
- Cope with stomach problems
- One serving per day proves beneficial for osteoporosis
- Increases the capacity to absorb the nutrients and minerals from other food stuffs
- Proven beneficial for the lactose intolerant as they can gain all the nutritive contents of milk through curd as bacteria present in it breaks down the lactose before it enters our body.
- Proven beneficial for those suffering from vaginal infections
- Good for strong bones and teeth as its calcium content is high
- Minimize the risk of high blood pressure
- Coping with high level of cholesterol becomes easier with the help of curd

▶ The active culture of curd has been found to be beneficial in case of constipation.

▶ Curd helps us feel fuller and is thus, a very good snack for the weight conscious.

How to consume curd?

It is not too difficult to consume curd as a whole, however, it can also be blended with other food. A serving of curd regularly with our lunch is beneficial. Curd mixed with 2 tbsp of rice and a pinch of salt tastes yummy. Curd compliments spicy food. For example; if we cannot take spicy gravy, we can add a spoonful of curd to it. It will not only reduce the spiciness but also add a new flavor to our food.

Having buttermilk prepared out of curd after the meals proves beneficial for digestion. Savory lassi is friendly to our GI tract. Just add some coriander leaves, turmeric powder, cinnamon, cayenne pepper, ginger and garlic. Sweet lassi is to be avoided as it causes mucus thickening. Naturopathy discourages curd combination with fruits as it can diminish the digestive fire, change our intestinal flora, produce toxins and causes sinus congestion, cold, cough and allergies. Naturopathy suggests avoiding congestive and digestive fire dampening foods like cold yogurt mixed with fruits. The ever tempting mango lassi is a no no in Naturopathy. The best way to consume curd is to have it unflavored, natural and at room temperature.

According to Naturopathy, curd should not be consumed at night and should be consumed when it is completely coagulated. Though it provides lot of health benefits, over consumption should be avoided. Make sure that we consume curd when it is very fresh. Fresh curd even tastes better.

Milk contains protein that is mostly indigestible. Most of the milk just passes through our GI just the way it is and leave with our feces. The digestible remnants of an 8 oz glass of milk take approximately 5 to 7 hours to digest. Curd however contains friendly bacteria that helps break strong polypeptide bonds and at least, leaves the protein chains in digestible state for our small intestine to digest. The chains are smaller. Our body certainly gains more amino acids locked into the chains. It takes just 2 to 3 hours to digest curd. Therefore curd is definitely a better way to ingest milk.

Powdered coffee 'creamer' is processed chemicals

Every single day, there are millions of us who wake up to our favorite aromatic coffee with sugar and creamer. For health reasons, some of us even do away with the sugar and have our coffee with just the creamer. We falsely believe that somehow with creamers alone our cup of coffee is healthier. We know sugar is bad. We know that condensed milk is bad. What about creamers? What do we know about creamers? What are creamers?

Do we know that most coffee creamer products contain no actual cream, or real food for that matter, and it is really nothing more than a deceitful blend of toxic chemicals? These are, actually damaging powdered coffee additives. We can clearly say that, creamers are an overlooked detrimental element in our coffee.

When powdered coffee creamers were originated, it actually contained real dehydrated cream and sugar. The initial idea of dehydrating cream was to make it a non-perishable and convenient source of cream for coffee. As time went by, however, manufacturers began to phase out the cream, and replaced it with ingredients like processed vegetables oils, stabilizers, chemical sweeteners, and other additives that were less expensive and more easily dissolved in coffee. These artificial creamers made coffee taste better and were immediately accepted by consumers – yes, that's us. Now, creamers have become an important item not only in our grocer's list but also in our lives.

Fact – a sachet of so-called "creamer" substitute contains not a trace of actual food, at least not food in the technical sense of the word. For example, take the famous Coffee-Mate brand of coffee creamer; the creamer contains corn syrup solids, hydrogenated vegetable oils, and a handful of stabilizing, emulsifying, and flavoring chemicals. Not only is there no "cream" of any kind in Coffee-Mate's Original Powder, but there are also no natural food ingredients whatsoever.

Most creamers have Hydrogenated oils and Corn syrup which are highly-toxic 'non-foods' material. Technically both are NOT considered as food even though they are derived from real food. Corn syrup solids are chemically treated with hydrochloric acid. The resulting liquid remnant is then processed again and dried to form dried crystals. On the other hand, hydrogenated oils are produced using a series of chemical processes that involve various chemical treatments. The final product is the trans-fat, linked to heart disease and other complications

The other contents in creamers are also sodium caseinate, a milk derivative; mono- and diglycerides; sodium aluminosilicate; and artificial flavorings, all of which are non-foods as well. All of these have gone through intense chemical extrusions and alteration processes with chemical additives and are produced specifically for use in creamers, processed food items, laundry detergents, and other dry, powdered products.

Dairy is the best option. There are also some great non-dairy alternatives to conventional creamer products which include liquid coconut creamers, fresh coconut cream or milk and homemade almond milk. In comparison, condensed milk (not sweetened creamer) can be considered better than creamer. Read the labels carefully though. Avoid and refrain from all 3 in 1 coffee and tea varieties. Almost all of them contain these artificial additives. We have 2 in 1 sachets where sugar is omitted. With that, if creamer too is removed, then all we have is plain coffee. So, good old black coffee is always the best and healthier option.

Understanding SALT

Naturopathy practitioners have maintained for ages that iodized salt is factory made commercial salt and sea salt or rock salt is what the body requires. No wonder in the olden days, HBP problem was never heard of. We did not have iodized salt.

We need salt in everything we cook. Salt is the most vital ingredient in any recipe. But do we pay attention to the salt we eat? Is salt bad?

Bad salt is iodized salt which is fake salt. It's made up of only 3 synthetic chemicals – sodium, chloride and iodine. Iodized salt does not dissolve in water and neither does it dissolves in our body. Most importantly, it does not dissolve in our kidneys. However, this is the salt favored by many of us and strongly promoted by its manufacturers who say it is very clean and sanitized pointing to how white it is and how it glistens like diamonds. This fake salt is man-made in a factory. Isn't salt supposed to be natural?

Real salt comes from the sea and is dried under the sun and is commonly called Rock salt. Rock salt has more than 80 natural minerals including the 3 found in fake salt. Rock salt dissolves in water, dissolves in our body, dissolves in our kidneys and does not give us kidney stones. Contrary to the fact that salt raises BP, rock salt actually brings down blood pressure and prevents muscle cramps, numbness and the uncomfortable tingling feeling that follows numbness.

People, who suffer from cramps in the lower legs especially at night and during cold weather, need to take half teaspoon of rock salt with a glass of water. The relief from the excruciating pain is almost immediate. – www.tammmf.org

Salt is very important to our body. Without salt, our body cannot retain water no matter how much water we drink. We will still suffer dehydration because there will frequent urination and constant sweating.

Pay conscious attention to the salt we buy. Keep in mind that iodized salt is made in the factory and sea salt or rock salt is what our body requires.

Refined Salt:

Sodium	≈39%
Chloride	≈60%
Ferrocyanide, Aluminum Silicate, Ammonium Citrate, Dextrose	Up to 2%
Iodide	.01%

Datuk Ann Marianthony

Rock Salt:

Hydrogen	H	0.30 g/kg	Aluminum	Al	0.661 ppm	Chromium	Cr	0.05 ppm
Lithium	Li	0.40 g/kg	Silicon	Si	<0.1 g/kg	Manganese	Mn	0.27 ppm
Beryllium	Be	<0.01 ppm	Phosphorus	P	<0.10 ppm	Iron	Fe	38.9 ppm
Boron	B	<0.001 ppm	Sulfur	S	12.4 g/kg	Cobalt	Co	0.60 ppm
Carbon	C	<0.001 ppm	Chloride	Cl-	590.93 g/kg	Nickel	Ni	0.13 ppm
Nitrogen	N	0.024 ppm	Potassium	K+	3.5 g/kg	Copper	Cu	0.56 ppm
Oxygen	O	1.20 g/kg	Calcium	Ca	4.05 g/kg	Zinc	Zn	2.38 ppm
Flouride	F-	<0.1 g/kg	Scandium	Sc	<0.0001 ppm	Gallium	Ga	<0.001 ppm
Sodium	Na+	382.61 g/kg	Titanium	Ti	<0.001 ppm	Germanium	Ge	<0.001 ppm
Magnesium	Mg	0.16 g/kg	Vanadium	V	0.06 ppm	Arsenic	As	<0.01 ppm
Gold	Au	<1.0 ppm	Selenium	Se	0.05 ppm	Thulium	Tm	<0.001 ppm
Mercury	Hg	<0.03 ppm	Bromine	Br	2.1 ppm	Ytterbium	Yb	<0.001 ppm
Thallium	Ti	<0.06 ppm	Rubidium	Rb	<0.04 ppm	Lutetium	Lu	<0.001 ppm
Lead	Pb	<0.10 ppm	Strontium	Sr	<0.014 g/kg	Hafnium	Hf	<0.001 ppm
Bismuth	Bi	<0.10 ppm	Ytterbium	Y	<0.001 ppm	Tantalum	Ta	1.1 ppm
Polonium	Po	<0.001 ppm	Zirconium	Zr	<0.001 ppm	Wolfram	W	<0.001 ppm
Astatine	At	<0.001 ppm	Niobium	Nb	<0.001 ppm	Rhenium	Re	<2.5 ppm
Thorium	Th	<0.001 ppm	Molybdenum	Mo	<0.01 ppm	Francium	Fr	<1.0 ppm
Protactinium	Pa	<0.001 ppm	Technetium	Tc	N/A unstable isotope	Radium	Ra	<0.001 ppm
Uranium	U	<0.001 ppm	Ruthenium	Ru	<0.001 ppm	Actinium	Ac	<0.001 ppm
Rhodium	Rh	<0.001 ppm	Barium	Ba	1.96 ppm	Samarium	Sm	<0.001 ppm
Palladium	Pd	<0.001 ppm	Lanthanum	La	<0.001 ppm	Europium	Eu	<3.0 ppm
Silver	Ag	0.031 ppm	Cerium	Ce	<0.001 ppm	Gadolinium	Gd	<0.001 ppm
Cadmium	Cd	<0.01 ppm	Praseodymium	Pr	<0.001 ppm	Terbium	Tb	<0.001 ppm
Indium	In	<0.001 ppm	Neodymium	Nd	<0.001 ppm	Osmium	Os	<0.001 ppm
Tin	Sn	<0.01 ppm	Promethium	Pm	N/A unstable isotope	Iridium	Ir	<2.0 ppm
Antimony	Sb	<0.01 ppm	Dysprosium	Dy	<4.0 ppm	Platinum	Pt	<0.47 ppm
Tellurium	Te	<0.001 ppm	Holmium	Ho	<0.001 ppm	Cesium	Cs	<0.001 ppm
Iodine	I	<0.1 g/kg	Erbium	Er	<0.001 ppm			

The God given Freebies...........

And lastly, we have with us, a number of free Doctors waiting to be fully utilized................

These Doctors are most crucial for our healthy lifestyle. They are with us all the time but we are not using them although there is no consultation fee, appointments or expensive prescriptions.

1. **SUNLIGHT** – Our first doctor. The existence of life on earth is fueled by sunlight. The body produces vitamin D from sunlight and excessive seclusion from the sun can lead to deficiency unless adequate amounts are obtained through diet. Vitamin D is essential for strong bones because it helps the body use calcium from our diet. Make time to expose ourselves to this natural sauna. It's free.

2. **WATER** – Drink adequate amount of water every day. It is needed to replenish all the liquids of our body. H_2O is oxygen to trillions of cells in our body. Our system thrives on water. Water is the greatest detoxifying agent ever discovered. And it's free.

3. **AIR** – Breathing is Life. Consciously breathing for ten minutes invigorates every cell in our body. Our present consistently desperate lifestyle has resulted in grave disproportion between the hectic intellectual mind and our need to rest and relax our being as a whole. Deep breathing is a must to exhale all carbon and take in all oxygen in a clean and open environment. It's a luxury to breathe fresh air. Holding a breath and then releasing it clears all negativities in our body and harmonizes with nature and existence. (https://www.dhyanvimal.com/mastersbreath) It's free.

4. **DIET** – Eat nature's produce grown in our backyard. Grow our favorite fruit and vegetable. Include moringa in our meals. Nature has plenty of choice, choose what suits us best. We need not be a vegan for health. Organically produced vegetable and fruit from our backyard gives amazing benefits to our body in producing enzymes that protect every cell in our body. We are more herbivores by nature not carnivorous. Our meal should comprise of 20% meat and 80% fruits and vegetable. Our digestive system becomes sluggish with too much meat. Meat takes away 70% of our digestive energy. So be moderate with meat. Have moringa at hand at any time and include it all our cooking. It's free.

5. **EXERCISE** – No food can be 100% consumed without the corresponding arrangements to digest the same. Our body must move. Simple movement too is a great exercise. More important, is stretching the body which should start when waking up in the morning. And continue to be physically vibrant throughout the day. Stretching is essential as it helps our joints extent to their full range of movement and motion. Stretching also increases blood flow to our muscles effectively. Exercise in a proper state of mind and not under stress or duress. Relaxation is the reason for exercising a healthy state of mind. Exercise should not be rushed. Now housework.......... is NOT an exercise, it's a chore. Our body must activate with our consciousness. And it's also free.

6. **WALKING** - Every Organ of our body has its sensory nerve that ends at the bottom of our foot. If these points were massaged, we will feel instantly relaxed. Even tired, aching body gets instant relief when the foot is massaged. Acupressure studies cover this in great details. God has designed and created our body perfectly. He made us walk so that there will always be pressure on all our pressure points at the feet thus, keeping our organs activated all the time. So, let's keep walking. Isn't this amazing? And it's free.

7. **REST** – the most important part of health. We cannot physically and mentally function without proper rest. Deep sleep is compulsory for regenerative activities. Physical and mental performance suffers with inadequate sleep. Our relationships too suffer when we deprive ourselves of rest. Diseases develop because we have not given our body

enough time (rest) to repair damaged tissues. Just putting up our feet is an excellent way to rest and relax most of the musculature of our body. And it is absolutely free.

8. **POSITIVE ATTITUDE** – absolute for happiness and joy. A positive attitude helps us cope better with everything in our life. It brings about optimism in things that we do in our daily life, and makes it easier to avoid worries and negativity. If we adopt it as a way of life, it will bring constructive changes into our life, and makes us happier, brighter and more successful. With a positive attitude we see the brighter side of life, become optimistic, and expect the best to happen. It certainly is a state of mind that is well worth developing, cultivating and practicing. And this too can be done for free.

9. **WAKE UP VERY EARLY IN THE MORNING** – In order to put our life in order. "Early to bed and early to rise makes us healthy, wealthy as well as wise". And that is not just an age-old saying. It worked then and it will definitely work now. Sleep is an important factor in health but waking up early is an even more important beneficial factor for our body and mind.

Waking up early gives us the time to exercise. We can easily go for a jog, do a few laps in the pool, practice yoga or hit the gym at a relaxed pace with plenty of time at hand.

Spend 15 minutes on meditation. The primary benefit of meditation is stress relief. The deep rest experienced during this practice of Meditation allows the body to naturally dissolve stress and strain. After meditating it is common for mediators to feel less stressed and are also able to deal more calmly with tense situations. When stress is reduced in the nervous system during meditation, benefits like better sleep and clearer thinking also naturally develops. Many research studies have verified that the daily practice of meditation produces a wide range of positive effects on our mind, body, and behavior. There is nothing like beginning the day with a dose of meditation. It will help calm our mind and sharpen our reflexes to keep us going through our busy schedule of work. Only an early morning person knows the calmness and serenity that those hours offer. The silence, the birds chirping, the absence of cars honking, and the sunrise are all advantages only early rising can offer.

It is a known fact that early risers are more prone to be productive and efficient at work. In fact, students who wake up earlier than usual are known to get higher grades than those who wake up late and rush.

We are able to sit down and savor the first meal in a relaxed state. It gives us ample time to get ready on time, and we suffer less stress. We are able to beat the traffic and drive to work at ease. All we need to do is get into the routine habit of rising early. Once we are able to set a routine, our life will obviously lead to better productivity not only at work, but also at home and as an individual.

We feel happier, lighter and somehow more optimistic when we wake up early. The ones who wake up late morning or early afternoon are known to suffer depression, insomnia and pessimism. The bright start with exercise and optimism is bound to keep us feeling energized and optimistic all day. Proper routine and exercise are known factors in ensuring better health in the long run. Waking up early enables us to set aside time to plan out our day. Late risers lack the advantage of time for this important part of managing our day.

The benefits of waking up early are countless. It doesn't take much to change our lifestyle to acquire these benefits. After all, personal and professional well-being, and ultimate success are what all of us seek. So, why not adopt a healthier way of living and reap those benefits? So, let's rise early to kick-start the day. Of course, this too is free.

Lets Jolt Our Memory a Little

Nutritional discoveries are an on-going process. These findings have had a positive effect on our health and well-being since the time of Hippocrates. Nutrition and Nutrients are substances that are essential to life and must be acquired by only food.

It is important for us to understand nutrition. Today more than ever, obtaining nutritional knowledge can make a big difference in our lives. The market is saturated with all types of nutritional supplements. Every product is competing with another. Just when we think, we have purchased the best product; another "miracle" product comes by and confuses us further.

Modern farming techniques have depleted our soils of vital minerals. The widespread use of food additives, chemicals, sugar, fillers and healthy fats in our diets contributes to many of the degenerative diseases of modern day such as cancer, heart diseases, arthritis and osteoporosis and many more.

Let's take a look at the brief history of the science that offers us the hope of improving our health naturally......

400 B.C. – Hippocrates, the "Father of Medicines", said to his students, "Let Thy Food Be Thy Medicine and Thy Medicine Be Thy Food". He also said that a wise man should consider that good health is the greatest of human blessings

400 B.C. – Foods were often used as cosmetics or as medicines in the treatment of wounds. In some of the early Far-Eastern biblical writings, there were references to food and health. One story describes the treatment of eye disease, now known to be due to a vitamin A deficiency, by squeezing the juice of liver onto the eye. Vitamin A is stored in large amounts in the liver.

1500 – Scientist and Artist Leonardo Da Vinci compared the process of metabolism in the body to the burning of a candle.

1747 – Dr. James Lind, a physician in the British Navy, performed the first scientific experiment in nutrition. At that time, sailors were sent on long voyages for years and they developed scurvy (a painful, deadly, bleeding disorder) only non-perishable foods such as dried meat and breads were taken on the voyages, as fresh food wouldn't last. In his experiment, Dr. Lind gave some of the sailors sea water, others vinegar and the rest limes. Those given limes were saved from scurvy. As vitamin C was not discovered until the 1930s, Dr. Lind did not know it was the vital nutrient. As a note, British sailors became known as Limey.

1770 – Antoine Lavoisier, the Father of Nutrition and Chemistry discovered the actual process by which food is metabolized. He also demonstrated where animal heat comes from. In his equation, he describes the combination of food and oxygen in the body, and the resulting giving off of heat and water.

Late 1700's - a brilliant young French scientist, Antoine Lavoisier, became the "Father of Nutrition" from his brilliant work in chemistry. He put weight measures into chemistry, designed a calorimeter which measured the heat produced by the body from work and consumption of varying amounts and types of foods, and is famous for the statement "Life is a chemical process" (in French). He was elected to the French Academy of Science at age 24, and would have gone on to even greater scientific accomplishments, but was from an aristocratic family at the time in France when it was unpopular to be. He was beheaded in the French Revolution in 1794.

Early 1800 – It was discovered that foods are composed primarily of four elements: carbon, nitrogen, hydrogen and oxygen, and methods were developed for determining the amount of these elements.

1840 – Justus Liebug of Germany, a Pioneer in early plant growth studies, was the first to point out the chemical makeup of carbohydrates, fats and proteins. Carbohydrates were made of sugars, fats were fatty acids and proteins were made up of amino acids.

1897 – Christiaan Eijkmann, a Dutchman working with natives in Java, observed that some of the natives developed a disease called Beriberi, which caused heart problems and paralysis. He observed that when chickens were fed the native diet of white rice, they developed the symptoms of Beriberi. When he fed the chickens unprocessed brown rice (with the outer bran intact), they did not develop the disease. Eijkman then fed brown rice to his patients and they were cured. He discovered that food could cure diseases. Nutritionist later learned that the outer rice bran contains vitamin B1, also known as thiamine.

1912 – E. V. McCollum, while working for the U.S. Department of Agriculture at the University of Wisconsin, developed an approach that opened the way to the widespread discovery of nutrients. He decided to work with rats rather than large farm animals like cows and sheep. Using this procedure, he discovered the first fat soluble vitamin, Vitamin A. He found that rats fed with butter were healthier than those fed lard, as butter contains more Vitamin A.

1912 – Dr. Casmir Funk was the first to coin the term Vitamins as vital factors in the diet. He wrote about these unidentified substances present in the food, which could prevent the diseases of scurvy, Beriberi and pellagra (a disease caused by a deficiency of niacin, vitamin B3). The term vitamin is derived from the words vital and amine, because vitamins are required for life and they were originally thought to be amines – compounds derived from ammonia.

1930 – William Rose discovered the essential amino acids, the building blocks of protein.

1940 – The water soluble B and C vitamins were identified.

1940 – Russell Marker perfected a method of synthesizing the female hormone progesterone from a component of wild yams called diosgenin.

1950 – the present – The roles of essential nutrients as part of bodily processes have been brought to light. For example, more became known about the role of vitamins and minerals as components of enzymes and hormones that work within the body.

> *1968 – Linus Pauling, a Nobel prize winner in chemistry, created the term Orthomolecular Nutrition. Orthomolecular is, literally, "pertaining to the right molecule". Pauling proposed that by that by giving the body the right molecules in the right concentration (optimum nutrition), nutrients could be used by people to achieve better health and prolong life. Studies in the 1970s and 1980s conducted by Pauling and colleagues suggested that very large doses of vitamins C given intravenously could be helpful in increasing the survival time and improving the quality of life of terminal cancer patients.*

If we observe well, all of these founders, found the cure in the food. The cure had been in the food and still is. We are supposed to eat whole food and yet we go buy extracts. We spit out the seeds from grapes but we buy expensive grape seed extracts. The best form of extraction takes place in the stomach. That's the way we are designed.

Taking dietary supplements has become the trend these days – a universal adoption. All of us at one point of time brag about the supplements that we take. We talk about the price (the pricier the better), quality, brand and the origin. Supplements are "supplements" and it is not complete food. It is only meant to supplement our food. Now, why do we need to take an inadequate meal in the first place? If a meal is complete, then supplements are unnecessary. Therefore, we need to consciously put together a total meal that provides us with everything that we need.

Dietary supplements are not intended to treat, diagnose, mitigate, prevent, or cure disease. In some cases, dietary supplements may have unwanted effects, for which there is a "warning" on the label that says, "If *symptoms persist, discontinue administration and consult your physician*". Our supplements abandon when there is a negative effect. But whatever our choices are, supplements should not replace the variety of foods that are most important to a healthful diet.

There are a number of factors that may influence our buying decision for supplements. Dietary supplements are available without a prescription through a number of retail outlets including grocery stores, drug stores, general merchants, retailers, natural food stores and specialty health and nutrition stores. Many dietary supplements can also be purchased online through the Internet.

But, many of us buy our supplements from Multi Level Marketing Companies. These MLM Companies sell their products to us using their members. These members are well trained by the Company just to sell. They are so good at selling their product to us, that we don't even look at the label that very clearly says, "*This product is not intended to diagnose, treat, cure, or prevent any disease*".

In science, credit goes to the man who convinces the world, not the man to whom the idea first occurs.
- FRANCIS GALTON —

Almost all of the MLM Companies either make misleading statements that could frighten us into taking dietary supplements that we had never actually needed prior to this or make unsubstantiated claims that their products would prevent or cure certain health problems. Some agents amplify the superiority of their product compared to ones in the retail outlets which are much cheaper.

Remember, all health products in the market go through the same processing procedures to qualify for the market. The word "research" for so many numbers of years is constantly mentioned although there would never be sufficient backups to substantiate these claims. They make statements about the biochemical properties of various substances without placing them in proper perspective. We are further deceived with statements like, there is a certain important nutrient that the body needs and only this one product has it. He omits the fact that people who eat sensibly have no valid reason to take a supplement.

MLM Companies have their distributors in the forefront. These distributors are told not to make claims for the products except for those found in company literature. However, many companies hold sales meetings at which people are encouraged to tell their story to the others in attendance. The "success" of network marketing lies in the enthusiasm of its participants. People who give such testimonials are usually motivated by a sincere wish to help their fellow humans. Since we tend to believe what others tell us about personal experiences, these testimonials become powerful persuaders.

When we are skeptical at times, the distributor would argue that the apparent benefits of "believing" in the products outweigh the risks involved. Do we need false beliefs in order to feel healthy? Do we need to believe that something can help us when in fact it is worthless? Sometimes, we do feel better when we take some supplement for the first time. This could be the placebo effect. Placebos do NOT have any active substance in them that can favorably affect our health. We could be taking a supplement that temporarily masks our conditions.

Extracts Misunderstood

When we hear the word "extracts", we tend to believe that our benefits are multi-folds. Do we understand what an extract really means? Where a large proportion of extractable material is obtained from a certain herbal material, the extract ratio will be low. For example, a ratio of 2:1 indicates that 50% of the extractable matter is obtained from the herb. This is the final extract. (E.g. 2 kg of herb will provide 1kg of extract). However, when only a small amount of extractable material is obtained using a particular extraction profile, the original extract ratio will be high (e.g. an original Extract Ratio of 20:1 indicates that only 5% of extractable components are obtained). E.g. 20 kg of herb is required to obtain 1 kg of original extract.

These extracts are marketed in a manner that implies that they are 'better' because they are derived from a larger quantity of raw herbal material. However the fact that these extracts are also diluted with a carrier or diluents, for a variety of purposes is not revealed.

High numbers thrown in during sales presentations for supplements like, "500 to 1 Extract" or something like that - does NOT mean that this product is 500 times more concentrated than ordinary herb, and that by some silly logic such "highly concentrated Extract" is "Stronger", and thus more effective, giving faster and better results. There is no scientifically accepted determination of what a 500 to 1 extract is. Any company that claims they are selling a product that is even 200 times as potent as the regular powder is misleading us. We are not being super-smart by consuming highly concentrated foods because it really is unnecessary as this only reflects the proportion of how much raw herb material has been used to produce 1 lot of final product. It does not mean that it wasn't diluted with carrier (or solvent) or mixed with some other additives or fillers. So such "Extracts" are not "better" or "stronger" or "more effective" than just an ordinary herb.

Even herbs like root - after cutting off unnecessary parts, stripping it of skin, cutting into chips, drying up, grinding into powder can be considered "extracts" as they are in the purest form. But not products called and marketed as "extracts" or "herbal extracts" that - are processed and further processed through the extraction techniques and with some solvents, with some added carriers and excipients and yet again possibly further diluted before being finally sold to consumer. Thus, they are NOT "better" or "stronger" than original (raw one) or processed herb ("extracts").

Purchasing Dietary Supplements

We are constantly reminded never to self diagnose any health condition. We are instructed to work with our health care provider to determine how best to achieve optimal health and always check with our health care provider before taking a supplement, especially when combining or substituting them with other foods or medicine. Now, who is our health care provider? The nice doctor whom we trust because we had visited him a few times? Doctors are from illness industry not wellness. If we ask him about illness and medication, he knows. But when it comes to wellness, he too needs help just like us.

Unknowingly, for ages we had surrendered our health to our Doctors. The only person who knows us well enough is us. Nobody knows us better than us. Doctors are our illness experts and they have very little to do with wellness.

An observation by the Indian Medical Association's (IMA) Pune chapter says that an Indian doctor's average lifespan is 57 years, more than 10 years lesser than that of the general population.

Nobody actually conducts an in-depth test on these products that we pay so much for. Who are we to seek if we had questions about the product? Do we ask the manufacturer? Of course Google had always been at hand when we had questions. Even then, Google too gives us many different contradicting versions of answers.

There are a few independent organizations that offer "hologram seal of approval" that is displayed on the products. This only indicates that the product has passed the organization's quality tests for things such as potency and contaminants. These "seals of approval" do not mean that the product is safe or effective; they provide assurance that the product was properly manufactured, that it contains the ingredients listed on the label and that it does not contain harmful levels of contaminants. That's it.

Supplements are processed. Why do we say that processed food is bad for us yet, we are obsessed with Supplements?

For additional details; www.tammmf.org